TO SANDRA, MONTY, AND BRUCE

SAMUEL GOMPERS
Founder of AFL
Courtesy of AFL-CIO News

LABOR RELATIONS AND THE SUPERVISOR

M. GENE NEWPORT

Professor of Management
The Municipal University of Omaha

ADDISON-WESLEY PUBLISHING COMPANY

READING, MASSACHUSETTS · MENLO PARK, CALIFORNIA
LONDON · DON MILLS, ONTARIO

This book is in the

ADDISON-WESLEY SERIES IN SUPERVISION

Consulting Editor

William C. Christensen

 Printed in the United States of America. Published simultaneously in Canada. Library of Congress Catalog Card No. 68-19343.

PREFACE

Unions have grown rapidly since employees were granted the right to organize and bargain collectively under the National Labor Relations Act (Wagner Act) of 1935. As a result of this growth, unions now exert a powerful influence on the day-to-day operations of many businesses. This is felt particularly at the supervisory level in areas such as hiring, firing, wages, hours, discipline, and working conditions.

As members of management closest to employees, supervisors play a vital role in developing and maintaining healthy labor-management relationships. In order to be most effective in this role, supervisors must understand union goals and practices, certain areas of labor legislation, labor-management contracts, and methods for dealing with grievances. This book is designed to aid supervisors in acquiring a working knowledge of these and other important areas in the field of labor relations. Questions for discussion and a suggested bibliography are included at the end of each chapter and the appendix contains short quizzes, each with its own scoring key.

Another text, also in the Addison-Wesley Supervisory Series, is a programed workbook on *Labor Relations for the Supervisor,* prepared by Professors Joseph P. Yaney and Geary A. Rummler of the University of Michigan. Their book provides an excellent opportunity for self-instruction: the supervisor can answer questions or study short cases dealing with many important matters concerning labor relations. He can then check his answers against those given in the text in order to determine how much he has learned about a particular topic. Through the knowledge and skill gained from these two books, we hope that each supervisor will be able to deal with his own special labor problems in the most efficient and effective manner.

ACKNOWLEDGMENTS

My thanks are extended to Dean John W. Lucas of the College of Business Administration, and to Dr. Jack A. Hill, Head, Department of Management, The Municipal University of Omaha. Their continued interest and assistance helped an idea become a reality. In addition, my family deserves special thanks. Several family outings were graciously postponed while I worked to bring this book to its completion.

Omaha, Nebraska M.G.N.
January, 1968

CONTENTS

1
Union Growth and Development

Unions have a long history in the United States. In fact, some associations of skilled workers existed even before the Declaration of Independence in 1776. However, these associations were small and were formed primarily to provide an opportunity for workers to meet and to seek solutions for their common problems.

Around the beginning of the 1800's, workers in several trades began to organize local groups similar to modern unions. These groups bargained with employers over matters such as wages, hours, apprenticeship regulations, and an early form of the closed shop. Shoemakers, tailors, carpenters, and printers were among the earliest groups to form organizations of this type.

Although these early unions were small and somewhat unstable, they often used the strike to seek their goals. In 1786, Philadelphia printers went on strike to gain a minimum wage of six dollars a week. Other strikes took place over such issues as a ten-hour day, additional pay for overtime, and the closed shop. Sympathy strikes were also seen at this time along with the creation by some unions of permanent strike funds.

A PERIOD OF SLOW GROWTH

Union growth experienced many ups and downs during most of the 1800's, and progress was quite slow until about the time of the Civil War. Several factors were responsible for this delay. Some of the more important ones are discussed below.

Economic Conditions

Four periods of economic depression during the sixty-five years between 1815 and 1880 caused a great lag in union growth. Unions advanced and prospered during the economic upswings between depressions. However, during the depressions, membership fell off and many unions were wiped out or seriously weakened. This rise and fall of membership continued until the 1880's when labor organizations finally gained enough strength to survive depressions.

Changing Union Objectives

Unions changed objectives quite frequently during the 1800's. Such changes were closely related to economic conditions. When business conditions were good, unions stressed collective bargaining on wages, hours, and the protection of craft lines. The major objectives would shift to the areas of political action and social reform, however, when the economy moved toward a period of depression. These goals would then remain until another upswing in the economy.

Due to the frequent shifting of objectives, changes occurred quite often in union membership. At one time, it would be made up almost entirely of skilled craftsmen. At another time, less skilled workers and farmers would be attracted to the ranks. As a result of such changes in constituency, unions had difficulty in building stable organizations during the early 1800's.

Immigration

Between 1820 and 1930, some 38 million immigrants entered the United States. Many arrived with little money and were willing to work at low wages in order to support themselves and their families. They were in a strange country and were often afraid and confused by what they saw. Thus many of these people gave little thought to the possible benefits of unionism during their first few years in America.

Immigrants also brought differences in language, race, custom, and education into the labor force. Such factors created additional problems for unions in their organization drives and contributed to slowing down the rate of their progress during this time.

The Movement of Workers

In addition to immigration, other factors caused the nature of the labor force to change quite often. The frontier was still open and people were moving west. Many who did not actually move refused to consider themselves as part of the working class. They still dreamed of moving and of being their own boss. Thus they were not interested in unions. These forces, and the movement of workers from one place to another, made it hard for unions to attract and hold members until the late 1800's.

Employer Resistance

During the 1800's and the early 1900's, employers resisted unions in various ways. They turned to the courts in many cases, and law suits were brought against the unions as criminal conspiracies. These suits stated that the organization and combination of unions would result in joint action harmful to the public. The courts ruled in favor of the employers in several of these cases. In addition, employers often obtained court orders to prevent strikes and other union actions.

The *yellow-dog* contract was also used during this time. Under this contract, the employee, when he was hired by a company, agreed not to join a union. Some union members were blacklisted, which meant they would not be hired by other companies. Other employees were fired for their union activities and were replaced with non-union help. These and other tactics were often reinforced through the combined efforts of employers who would join to fight a union.

Many employers felt their resistance was right. They believed that unions would reduce their control over the workers. On the other hand, unions believed their cause was just. Thus, the struggle continued and reached its peak with the company unions, strikebreaking, lockouts, and industrial spies of the early 1900's. It was finally brought under control by government legislation in the 1930's.

BEGINNING OF NATIONAL UNIONS

As early as the 1830's, there was a movement toward the development of national unions. At that time, unions of skilled workers in a common trade would often band together on a citywide basis to protect their job security and earnings. However, these city centrals soon recognized that if they were to maintain good conditions in one city, it was necessary for similar conditions to exist in other cities. Thus they saw the importance of tying local groups together through the formation of national unions.

The first attempt to organize union groups beyond the local level was made in 1834 with the formation of the National Trades' Union by several craft unions that were already organized on a citywide basis. A few other craft unions also tried to set up national unions during this time. However, these efforts failed with the coming of the financial crisis of 1837 and the depression of the 1840's.

At the time of the Civil War, unions started to grow again. By the late 1860's, about thirty national unions had been formed. These included organizations of printers, molders, stone cutters, machinists, and locomotive engineers. In 1866, the National Labor Union was organized in another attempt to unite labor groups throughout the country into one federation. This effort did not have much success and the National Labor Union was abandoned in 1872. Several of the national unions did survive, however, and union power slowly moved from the local to the national level.

KNIGHTS OF LABOR

The Noble Order of the Knights of Labor was founded by Philadelphia tailors in 1869 as a secret society. A few years later, this organization began to branch out to other cities and other trades, and its secret rituals gradually disappeared.

The Knights hoped to combine the members of existing craft unions with other skilled and unskilled workers to form "One Big Union." In a broad sense, membership was to include all who worked with hand or brain except for saloon keepers, stockbrokers, bankers, lawyers, and professional gamblers.

By the late 1870's, the Knights had become a national organization with a new constitution and a membership of close to 10,000. This figure had risen to approximately 100,000 by 1885. In that year, the Knights were successful in their strike against Jay Gould and his powerful railway system. As a result, they gained worldwide attention, and membership jumped to 700,000 during the next year.

The objectives of the Knights of Labor included an eight-hour day, elimination of child and convict labor, equal pay for equal work by women, public ownership of utilities, and the establishment of cooperatives. These goals attracted a wide range of people, and this diversity was largely responsible for the organization's decline. The skilled workers favored collective bargaining to advance their cause, while many of the unskilled workers felt that the Knights should use political action and social reform to achieve their goals. Such conflicts between the two groups were never reconciled and various craft unions began leaving the Knights in the middle 1880's. In addition, the Knights lost several strikes after their earlier victories. Membership began to fall. It dropped to 100,000 by 1890, and the Knights were no longer able to exert much power on the labor movement, although they remained on the scene until 1917.

AMERICAN FEDERATION OF LABOR (AFL)

As we have seen, the interests of the skilled workers in the labor movement were not the same as those of the unskilled laborers. Several craft unions had not joined the Knights of Labor for this reason. However, their leaders recognized the benefits of a national organization made up entirely of trade unions. The first steps in this direction were taken while the Knights were still in power. In 1881, the printers, iron and steel workers, molders, cigarmakers, carpenters, and glassworkers met with a mixture of other labor groups to form the Federation of Organized Trades and Labor Unions (FOTLU). Its leaders were Samuel Gompers and Adolph Strasser, both of the cigarmakers' union. Progress and growth were slow for the next five years as the FOTLU ran second to the Knights of Labor.

When the Knights met at their annual convention in 1886, they refused to respect the jurisdiction of the large national craft unions. Several of these unions then founded the American Federation of Labor. They were joined by the FOTLU, and Samuel Gompers was elected president of the new federation. Except for one year, he was to hold this office until his death in 1924.

The policies of the AFL were quite different from those of the Knights of Labor. There was no call for political action or social reform to improve the conditions of unskilled workers. Instead, the emphasis was upon collective bargaining for better wages, hours, working conditions, and other benefits for the skilled craftsmen.

The organization of the AFL was also in sharp contrast to that of the Knights of Labor. The Knights had favored a tight control over member organizations, a policy that had been resisted by the craft unions. Recognizing this fact, the AFL chose to let each national union handle its own affairs. Thus the new federation assumed the role of assisting the member unions rather than that of directing their actions.

The AFL began with a membership of approximately 140,000 and grew steadily as more and more craft unions accepted the goals and policies of the new organization. However, the old conflict of craft versus industrial unions was to accompany this growth. As industry expanded during the early 1900's, the problem became even greater. There were frequent demands to bring the growing number of unskilled workers into the ranks of the AFL. The ultimate outcome was the formation of the CIO in 1938.

CONGRESS OF INDUSTRIAL ORGANIZATIONS (CIO)

During the early 1930's the AFL did attempt to solve the problem of admitting industrial workers to its ranks. In 1934, the executive council of the federation was directed to issue charters to certain national and international unions of industrial workers. This effort did not satisfy those members of the AFL who favored the admission of industrial unions, however, since they preferred a much more aggressive campaign. As a result, six unions belonging to the AFL and the officers of two other AFL unions formed the Committee for Industrial Organizations (CIO). The purpose of the group was to promote the unionization of industrial workers. The committee would then try to get such unions to join with the American Federation of Labor.

The executive council of the AFL did not approve of the committee's actions and asked the group to disband. When the CIO failed to do so, the conflict continued and the unions within the committee were finally expelled from the AFL in May, 1938.

Meeting later in 1938, the Committee for Industrial Organization reorganized and became a federation of national and international unions under the name of the Congress of Industrial Organizations. The organization of the CIO was similar to that of the AFL. The member unions were given the authority to handle their own affairs with the CIO providing assistance when called upon.

While the conflict between craft and industrial unions did not end with the advent of the CIO, union growth was not harmed by the difficulties. Competition between the two groups led to more organizing efforts, and as a consequence total union membership increased at a very fast rate.

AFL-CIO

Several events took place during the forties and early fifties that led to a reduction of the conflict between the AFL and CIO and opened the door for a merger of the two groups. First, the AFL began to develop a new attitude toward the unionization of industrial workers. As several AFL unions admitted such workers to their ranks, the issue of craft versus industrial unions began to disappear.

Second, both the AFL and CIO had become more involved in political affairs during the years of their growth. However, their actions had not always been successful. When the Taft-Hartley Act was passed in 1947, both groups saw a need for more cooperation in the political area.

Third, the presidents of both groups died in 1953. This brought new men with new ideas to the top leadership of the two federations. In fact, both George Meany (AFL) and Walter Reuther (CIO) gave their officers the authority to work toward a merger shortly after they were elected to the presidency of their respective organizations.

GEORGE MEANY
President, AFL-CIO
Courtesy of AFL-CIO News

WALTER REUTHER
President, Auto Workers Union
Courtesy of AFL-CIO News

Fourth, the two groups approved a no-raiding agreement in 1953. This agreement stated that unions belonging to one group would not try to recruit or organize in a plant where a union of the other group had already established a bargaining relationship.

The no-raiding agreement was followed by continued efforts toward a merger which finally led to the writing of a new constitution. This constitution was approved by both groups in 1955 and resulted in the formation of the AFL-CIO. George Meany of the AFL was elected president of the new federation, and Walter Reuther of the CIO became a vice-president and headed the new Industrial Union Department that was created within the federation.

Structure of the AFL-CIO

The organizational structure of the AFL-CIO reflects the earlier belief of both groups that member unions should have the authority to handle their own affairs. Thus the federation does not call strikes or engage in collective bargaining. Instead, it deals with publicity, political affairs, research, and other similar activities that provide assistance to the member unions.

The Convention. An organization chart of the AFL-CIO is shown on page 14. By looking at the chart, one can see that the national convention is the top authority within the AFL-CIO. This group meets every two years to develop the guiding policies of the federation. The number of delegates to the convention from the national and international unions is determined by the size of each union. Other affiliated groups are entitled to be represented by one representative each.

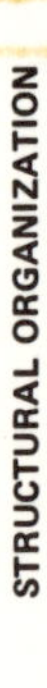

STRUCTURAL ORGANIZATION
of the
AMERICAN FEDERATION OF LABOR AND CONGRESS OF INDUSTRIAL ORGANIZATIONS

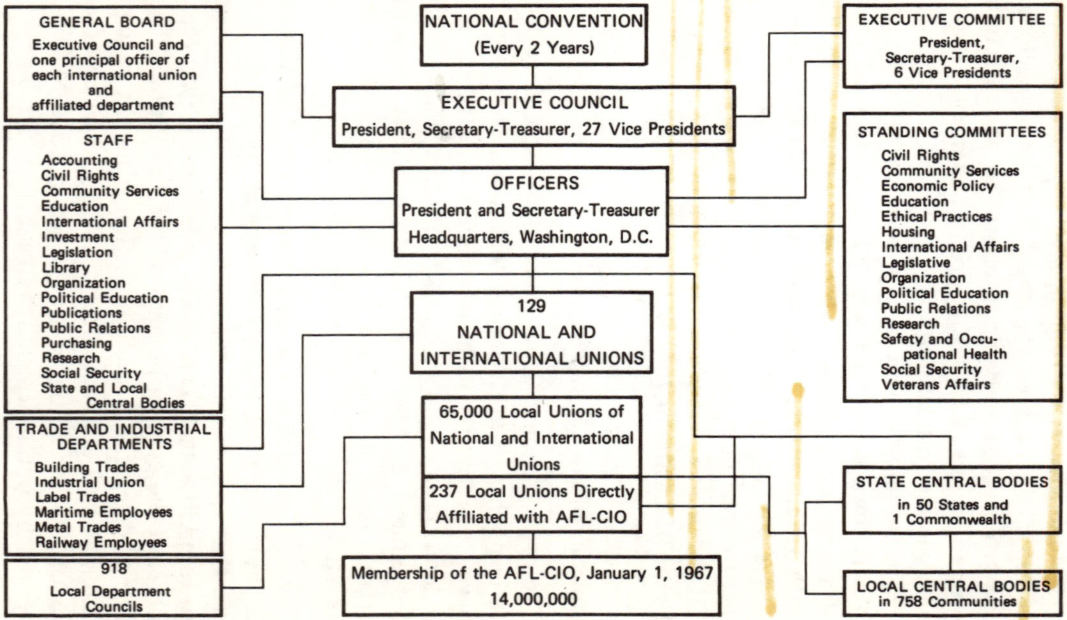

NATIONAL CONVENTION
(Every 2 Years)

EXECUTIVE COUNCIL
President, Secretary-Treasurer, 27 Vice Presidents

EXECUTIVE COMMITTEE
President,
Secretary-Treasurer,
6 Vice Presidents

GENERAL BOARD
Executive Council and
one principal officer of
each international union
and
affiliated department

OFFICERS
President and Secretary-Treasurer
Headquarters, Washington, D.C.

STANDING COMMITTEES
Civil Rights
Community Services
Economic Policy
Education
Ethical Practices
Housing
International Affairs
Legislative
Organization
Political Education
Public Relations
Research
Safety and Occupational Health
Social Security
Veterans Affairs

STAFF
Accounting
Civil Rights
Community Services
Education
International Affairs
Investment
Legislation
Library
Organization
Political Education
Publications
Public Relations
Purchasing
Research
Social Security
State and Local Central Bodies

129
NATIONAL AND
INTERNATIONAL UNIONS

STATE CENTRAL BODIES
in 50 States and
1 Commonwealth

LOCAL CENTRAL BODIES
in 758 Communities

TRADE AND INDUSTRIAL DEPARTMENTS
Building Trades
Industrial Union
Label Trades
Maritime Employees
Metal Trades
Railway Employees

65,000 Local Unions of
National and International
Unions

237 Local Unions Directly
Affiliated with AFL-CIO

918
Local Department
Councils

Membership of the AFL-CIO, January 1, 1967
14,000,000

Source: AFL-CIO, 1966.

Executive Council. The executive council is directly below the convention in the chain of authority. Its major purposes are to carry out the policies determined by the convention and to deal with issues that may arise between conventions.

Membership of the council includes the president, the secretary-treasurer, and twenty-seven vice-presidents of the AFL-CIO who are elected by a majority vote of the convention. Meetings of this group are held at least three times a year.

Executive Committee and General Board. The president and secretary-treasurer are next in the chain of command. They are responsible for supervising the affairs of the federation. Two other official groups assist them in their duties.

One is the executive committee which consists of the president, secretary-treasurer, and six vice-presidents who are selected by the executive council. This group meets every two months to advise and consult with the president and the secretary-treasurer on policy matters.

The second body is the general board which meets at least once a year to consider policy matters referred to it by the executive council and the executive officers. Membership includes all members of the executive council plus a chief officer from each affiliated national and international union. In addition, one person from each Trade and Industrial Department is a member of the board.

Staff Groups and Committees. The officers of the AFL-CIO are also assisted by a large number of professional staff groups and standing committees. These groups do much work in public relations, union organizing, political activities, worker education, and a host of other matters of concern to union members.

National and International Unions. The national and international unions are groups of local craft or industrial unions. They have major voting power in the AFL-CIO due to their large memberships. As a result, they can control the policies of the federation. Their association with the federation is voluntary and they may leave at any time. They have the authority to handle their own affairs with local unions. The AFL-CIO controls them only through influence or by threatening to expel or suspend them from the federation.

Local Unions. The strength of the federation rests with the local unions and their membership. Most of these locals are members of one of the national or international unions. However, some of them have avoided the national and international groups and have affiliated directly with the AFL-CIO.

Local unions operate under charters issued to them by the national or international organizations. They elect their own officers, negotiate contracts, conduct educational programs, admit members, collect dues, discipline members, and handle grievances or other matters of concern to local members.

The structure of the locals usually includes a president, vice-president, secretary, treasurer, executive board, stewards' body, and various committees. The stewards represent the local in its day-to-day contacts with the members. A local which deals with several small companies usually has a shop steward in each company. In larger plants, there are a number of stewards, since each is responsible to only one work unit or department. In either case the steward is an unpaid, elected union officer as well as a fellow worker.

The most important function of the steward is to handle grievances. He is usually very familiar with the union-management agreement since he must check grievances, present the member's complaint in grievance hearings, and seek to settle grievances through discussions with the foreman. Other duties of the steward include signing up members, telling them about meetings, gaining support for union programs, and getting members active in union affairs.

Departments and Local Department Councils. The various Trade and Industrial Departments are listed at the left of the chart. These departments represent the national unions whose members work together. They are grouped so that, for example, the national unions of carpenters, electricians, and other building trade unions would be included in the building trades department. By joining the departments, national unions can undertake joint actions in various areas. The departments also handle any jurisdictional disputes that arise when the members of two unions claim the right to do the same job.

The Department Councils are local offices of the Trade and Industrial Departments. As such, the councils function as links between the departments and the various local areas where problems arise.

State and Local Central Bodies. Members of the AFL-CIO may join state and local central bodies on a voluntary basis. These groups maintain staff groups and standing committees to deal with areas such as legislation, education, public relations, and other matters that affect union members.

The state and local bodies do not usually become involved in collective bargaining. Instead, they offer an opportunity for affiliated unions to become more active in various state and local affairs.

INDEPENDENT NATIONAL AND INTERNATIONAL UNIONS

While 14,000,000 employees, the large majority of all union members, belong to organizations affiliated with the AFL-CIO, there are approximately 3,000,000 other employees who belong to unaffiliated or independent unions. Some of these independents have been expelled from the Federation for various reasons. For example, the Teamsters Union has been an independent organization since it was expelled from the AFL-CIO in the 1950's. Other unaffiliated groups such as several of the railroad brotherhoods have never joined with the Federation. Still others, like the United Mine Workers, have changed back and forth from affiliated to unaffiliated standing.

SUMMARY

The early 1800's saw skilled workers forming associations similar to modern unions. The slow growth of these organizations was due to factors such as: (1) economic conditions; (2) changing union objectives; (3) immigration; (4) the movement of workers; and (5) employer resistance.

By the late 1860's, about thirty national unions had been established. Efforts to unite these and other labor groups into one federation led to establishing the National Labor Union in 1866. Although this association failed in 1872, union power was slowly moving from the local to the national level.

The Noble Order of the Knights of Labor was founded in 1869 to combine all workers into "One Big Union." By the middle 1880's, membership in this organization had reached approximately 700,000, but it soon fell to 100,000 because of internal conflicts, and the Knights were no longer able to influence the labor movement.

In 1886, several large craft unions, joined by the Federation of Organized Trades and Labor Unions, formed the AFL. Conflicts within this organization resulted in the formation of the CIO in 1938. Differences of opinion between the AFL and CIO were gradually reduced, however, and the two groups merged in 1955. The result is a complex structure that combines various local, state, national, and international groups into one federation – the AFL-CIO.

QUESTIONS FOR DISCUSSION

1. Why did business conditions and immigration have so much influence on the growth of unions during the 1800's? What conditions influence union growth at the present time? How?

2. Why did early unions often bargain for the closed shop? Are there similar reasons which help to explain some union actions at the present time?

3. Do you feel that it was right for employers to resist the formation of unions within their companies as they did before legislation prevented such actions? Why or why not?

4. Why has the issue of craft vs. industrial unions been so important to union growth and development? Is it still an issue?

5. What industrial unions are you familiar with? What craft unions are you familiar with? Are there any differences between the two groups?

6. Why do you feel unions have grown so much during the 1900's?

7. Why did the AFL and the CIO become more involved in political affairs as they grew in strength?

8. Why was the merger between the AFL and CIO so slow in coming about?

9. What benefits does a union gain through its affiliation with the AFL-CIO? Has anything happened in the last few years which would indicate that the marriage between the AFL and the CIO is not a happy one?

10. What do you think the future holds from the standpoint of further union growth and development?

SUGGESTED BIBLIOGRAPHY

Brief History of the American Labor Movement. Washington, D.C.: U.S. Government Printing Office, 1964.

Kuhn, Alfred. *Labor: Institutions and Economics.* New York: Harcourt, Brace and World, Inc., 1967, pp. 21-46.

Miernyk, William H. *The Economics of Labor and Collective Bargaining.* Boston: D.C. Heath and Company, 1965, pp. 13-57.

Yoder, Dale. *Personnel Management and Industrial Relations.* Englewood Cliffs, N.J.: Prentice-Hall, Inc., 1962, pp. 158-183.

2
Union Goals and Practices

Total union membership in the United States at the present time is approaching 17,000,000 or some 20% of the total labor force. Of this number, 14,000,000 belong to unions affiliated with the AFL-CIO, while more than 2,500,000 are members of unaffiliated unions. Within the AFL-CIO, the Automobile Workers (UAW) top the list with almost 1,200,000 members. Others in this group with more than 400,000 members each are the Steelworkers, Machinists, Electrical Workers (IBEW), Carpenters and Joiners, Hotel and Restaurant Employees, Ladies Garment Workers, Laborers', and Retail Clerks. The Teamsters (independent) is the largest of all unions with more than 1,500,000 members. For a complete list of national and international unions reporting a membership of 100,000 or more, see Table 2.1 on page 25.

During the past few years, increases in total union membership have come largely from members of the manufacturing industries, government employees, and white-collar workers. Continued economic growth and successful organizing efforts among government employees during the years of 1962-64 produced the largest growth that had occurred in union membership for nearly ten years. Organizing efforts are also continuing among groups such as teachers and certain farm workers (see Table 2.2). Although union membership has not kept pace with growth in the total labor force, advances are still being made and unions are here to stay.

The growth of union membership has often been hard for management to understand. In the past, it was not unusual for employers to fight unions as they sought to organize and attract new members. This approach led to so much violence it had to be halted by government legislation in the 1930's. A second approach has been called managerial paternalism where workers were given

Table 2.1

National and International Unions
Reporting 100,000 or More Members, 1964

Union	Members	Union	Member
Teamsters (Ind) ------	1,506,769	Textile Workers ------	177,000
Automobile Workers	1,168,067	Pulp, Sulphite --------	176,048
Steelworkers ----------	965,000	Letter Carriers --------	167,913
Machinists ------------	808,065	Retail, Wholesale-----	167,000
Electrical (IBEW) ----	806,000	Electrical (UE) (Ind) ---------------	165,000
Carpenters ------------	760,000	Rubber ----------------	164,661
Hotel & Restaurant--	444,581	Oil, Chemical ---------	162,000
Garment, Ladies'-----	442,318	Packinghouse ---------	145,000
Laborers' --------------	432,073	Ironworkers-----------	142,676
Retail Clerks ----------	427,555	Postal Clerks----------	139,000
Clothing Workers ----	377,000	Government (AFGE) -----------	138,642
Meat Cutters ----------	341,366	Bricklayers -----------	135,168
Building Service ------	320,000	Transport Workers --	135,000
Engineers, Operating	310,942	Transport Union -----	133,357
Communications Workers -----------	293,900	Papermakers ----------	133,000
Musicians -------------	275,254	Boilermakers----------	125,000
Electrical (IUE) ------	270,842	Maintenance of Way	121,151
Railway and Steamship Clerks -------	270,000	Railway Carmen -----	121,000
Plumbers --------------	255,765	Sheet Metal Workers	116,989
State, County ---------	234,839	Printing Pressmen----	115,589
Mine, District (50) (Ind) ---------------	210,000	Fire Fighters ---------	115,358
Painters ---------------	199,465	Typographical Union	113,453
Railroad Trainmen --	185,463	Teachers --------------	100,000

Source: Bureau of Labor Statistics, U.S. Department of Labor.

Table 2.2

Union Membership as a Percentage of Total Labor Force and of Employees in Nonagricultural Establishments

	Total union membership, excluding Canada (thousands)	Membership, excluding Canada, as a percentage of			
		Total labor force		Employees in nonagricultural establishments	
		Number (thousands)	Percent union members	Number (thousands)	Percent union members
1956	17,490	70,387	24.8	52,408	33.4
1957	17,369	70,744	24.6	52,894	32.8
1958	17,029	71,284	23.9	51,368	33.2
1959	17,117	71,946	23.8	53,279	32.1
1960	17,049	73,126	23.3	54,203	31.5
1961	16,303	74,175	22.0	53,989	30.2
1962	16,586	74,681	22.2	55,515	29.9
1963	16,524	75,712	21.8	56,643	29.2
1964	16,841	76,971	21.9	58,188	28.9

Source: Bureau of Labor Statistics, U.S. Department of Labor.

paid vacations, recreational programs, cafeterias, and other fringe benefits in an attempt to discourage them from wanting to join unions. Employees, however, were not given an opportunity to participate in deciding what benefits they would receive from management. Consequently, many workers felt that management was merely trying to buy their loyalty like the parent who lavishes his child with gifts and expects the child's love in return. As a result, employees continued to join the union movement where they saw an opportunity to satisfy their needs for security, recognition, belongingness, and self-expression which had been overlooked by management.

Today many employers find that their workers already are members of some labor groups, or they see organizing drives being conducted in their companies. In either case, a good labor-management relationship requires a knowledge and understanding of those goals and practices which continue to attract members to the union movement.

EARLY REFORM MOVEMENTS

All unions are involved with some type of reform since they seek to change conditions in the work-place. However, many early unions in this country were interested in a large number of reforms that went beyond the area of working conditions. The Knights of Labor were interested in the elimination of child and convict labor, in public ownership of utilities, and in the establishment of cooperatives whose members would share equally in the profits of the business. Other unions sought such things as free schools, different systems of taxation, and equal pay for equal work by women.

History has shown that unions have always had difficulty in attracting and holding members who were interested only in social reforms. In the past, unions could gain members during periods of economic depression when employees would see social reform as the best way to improve conditions and protect their security. This was especially true of the unskilled workers. In more prosperous times, employees were more interested in gaining better hours and wages. As a result, unions were forced to change goals quite often in order to maintain their membership. Those unions that did not change their objectives to meet the needs of members were often wiped out as employees left their ranks to seek greener pastures.

UNIONS OF TODAY

The American Federation of Labor learned a valuable lesson from the failures among unions whose major objective was social reform. Leaders of the AFL saw that the skilled workers in the union movement were most interested in collective bargaining to improve their job security, wages, hours, and other conditions of employment. Accordingly, they avoided social reform as one of their objectives and stressed the benefits to be gained through group action in dealing with employers. This way of thinking was very important to the growth and success of the AFL and the later AFL-CIO, and it remains as a major part of the philosophy of most unions at the present time.

Business Unions

Most organized labor groups in the United States began as business unions. They placed great emphasis on bargaining for better wages, hours, working conditions, and other matters related to employment. For this reason, they have often been called "Bread and Butter Unions."

The major goal of the business union has been to obtain for its members a good contract with management. When an agreement was reached, the union's job became one of seeing that the contract was enforced. In either case, members saw the union as a business agent who stood up for them in their dealings with management groups. Naturally, they were willing to pay dues for this service.

Business unions have done more than bargain over wages and hours. They have also established rules to guide the actions of both management and union in certain areas. They have, for example, outlined work rules and grievance procedures, spelling out the rights of all parties under the union contract. This aspect of their work has sometimes been referred to as defining civil rights in industry.

Welfare Unions

These groups have carried on the same work as business unions. They have bargained with management over economic issues such as wages and fringe benefits. Welfare unions have also attempted to play a part in dealing with community problems faced by their members. One of their major goals has been aiding members both on and off the job. As a result they have offered a variety of services to their members, sponsoring housing projects, cooperative stores, counseling services, recreational programs and credit unions.

Business-Welfare Unions

Welfare unions which offer services beyond those of the business union appear to obtain more loyalty from their members than do the business unions. Members can see the union working for them in the community as well as on the job. Although the cost of welfare unionism is high, the acceptance of such organizations seems to be growing. Consequently, health and welfare funds, adult education, recreation, and other programs are being offered to keep up with the changing interests of union members. And, as these interests continue to expand, we will undoubtedly see a continuing trend toward a combination of business and welfare unionism.

CURRENT UNION GOALS

Some goals of organized labor have been discussed in the examination of business and welfare unions. In order to understand why unions are able to attract and hold members, perhaps a more complete analysis of these and other goals is necessary. Let us examine them in more detail.

Economic Gain

Since the economic issues surrounding contract negotiations and strikes are brought to the general public by newspaper, radio, and television reporters, they are probably the goals most frequently associated with the labor movement. Collective bargaining focuses primarily on higher wage levels, payment for overtime, shorter hours, insurance coverage, pension plans, and paid vacations. The union seeks to keep wages commensurate with the cost of living, and attempts to relate wages to productivity increases. In short, emphasis is on a continuous betterment of the workers' standard of living.

Employee Security

In addition to better wages, hours, and fringe benefits, unions also seek additional security for their members. They fight for various annual wage plans which will guarantee the workers a known wage for at least one year, for wages based on the cost of living to protect their members from spiralling costs and inflation, and more recently for some form of permanent job security. They establish grievance procedures and agreements whereby they have the right to question discharges or disciplinary action taken against employees. They enforce seniority provisions for wage increases, opportunity for advancement, and recall to jobs after a layoff. Unions also have supported legislation concerned with unemployment benefits, social security, and other matters. Thus action by the unions may take many forms as they seek to provide more job security for their members.

Union Recognition

A major goal of all unions is to gain maximum strength in their dealings with management. Such strength in collective bargaining depends on the recognition held by the union. This recognition, in turn, is based on the employer's acceptance of the union as the representative for all workers in a bargaining unit.

A bargaining unit may include the members of a single craft line, or it can cover several jobs in a firm. Sometimes two or more unions may seek to represent portions of the same bargaining unit. In these cases, the National Labor Relations Board (NLRB) determines the rights of each union to represent certain employees. However, the NLRB takes action only when the dispute involves interstate business. Many states have labor relations boards to deal with the disputes entirely within state boundaries.

Obtaining the recognition of management is not the problem that it was before the National Labor Relations Act of 1935. This Act created the NLRB and gave it the authority to determine appropriate bargaining units. Thus, if a union does not receive voluntary recognition from an employer, the NLRB has the authority to name the union chosen by the employees as the certified bargaining agent.

Union Security

Unions must be confident when speaking for their membership. They must know what members expect from the union. Thus, unions seek various types of security which will give them maximum strength and authority in their dealings with management. Some forms of union security are discussed below.

Closed Shop. Under the closed shop, only union members in good standing can be hired. Furthermore, management agrees to obtain new employees from the union. Thus, the union is able to control the labor supply. Although the closed shop was outlawed by the Taft-Hartley Act, some contracts spell out procedures nearly as stringent. For this reason, the closed shop has been included as a form of union security.

Union Shop. When a contract provides for the union shop, nonunion employees may be hired, but must join the union if they stay after the close of a given period of time, usually thirty days. Although the union shop is very common, employers often dislike it since they feel some employees are forced to join and to pay dues against their will.

Right-to-work laws in some states prohibit the union shop. These laws state that the right to a job will not be denied to anyone because he fails to join the union or maintain membership. While there have been recent attempts to repeal right-to-work laws, the matter still is not settled. As a result, it appears that union shop agreements will be controversial issues for some time to come.

Agency Shop. In states having right-to-work laws, the closed shop, union shop, and maintenance of membership are prohibited. As a result, an employee can decide whether or not he wants to join a union. He is not required to join, as is the case under a union shop agreement.

Unions feel the right-to-work laws produce too many "free riders," employees who share the benefits obtained by collective bargaining, but who do not support the union. To avoid this situation, unions have bargained for agency shop agreements by which all employees must pay dues to the union although they do not have to join. At present, some states with right-to-work laws prohibit agency shops. Others have made no definite ruling on the matter and in those states the agency shop remains as a form of security for the union.

Preferential Shop. Recognition and security are granted to the union under this type of shop, since management agrees to give union members the first chance at employment. New employees are sought from a union's hiring hall. The employer looks to other sources for employees only when the hiring hall cannot provide the type of labor required for the job. While such preference is illegal under the Taft-Hartley Act, some contracts include clauses which ensure almost the same advantage.

Maintenance of Membership. Under this agreement, all employees who are union members on a specified date must maintain their membership during the term of the contract, and employees who join on or after the specified date must remain as members of the union during the term of the contract.

Dues Checkoff. At present, about sixty-five percent of all contracts provide for the checkoff. Under this arrangement, union members must authorize the employer to deduct union dues from their paychecks. The employer makes the deductions and sends the dues to the union. Initiation fees and other payments to the union may also be taken care of under this type of plan.

CURRENT UNION PRACTICES

Unions feel it is necessary to achieve goals such as those outlined above in order to hold present members while attracting new ones. In order to enforce demands for the benefit of their members they engage in the following practices.

Collective Bargaining

Management and the union determine the conditions of employment through collective bargaining. In the process, both parties have the opportunity of speaking out to gain advantages or to protect their interests. The union is, of course, interested in obtaining added benefits for its members plus security and recognition for the union as a whole. On the other hand, management is interested in protecting its prerogatives while resisting further demands. Thus agreements are usually reached only after much bargaining.

Strikes

Unions employ the strike to accomplish various objectives. These objectives are seen by examining different types of strikes. For example, an *economic strike* takes place when union members stop work to emphasize their demands for certain benefits. In an *unfair labor practices strike,* members stop working to protest what they feel is an unfair practice by management. Through the *sympathy strike,* members support union members who are on strike against other firms. When a sympathy strike includes most of the members of one union in a community, it is called a *general strike.*

Although a strike can put great economic pressure on an employer, the loss of wages during a strike also places a hardship on union members. For this reason, unions have created strike funds to provide financial assistance to their members during a strike. Depending upon the union involved, payments to members can range from emergency benefits, which are often substantially less than normal earnings, to amounts that are almost the same as regular earnings. In either case, however, a strike fund usually increases bargaining power since it eases the impact of immediate losses to union members.

While the right to strike is protected by law, there are some limitations. For example, if a strike is harmful to public health and safety, it may be designated a national emergency strike. In this case, legislation provides for a "cooling off" period during which the workers return to their jobs while efforts to reach an agreement are continued.

Picketing

Picketing takes place when union members parade with signs to show why they are on strike. Since members of other unions usually will not cross the picket lines, all work may come to a halt until the conflict is settled.

Boycotts

A boycott represents another economic weapon of the union. A primary boycott occurs when the union enjoins its members not to buy from a business where there is a labor dispute. This type of boycott is legal under present legislation, but it is effective, of course, only against employers who deal directly with the public.

A secondary boycott goes one step further. In this case, other firms may be boycotted because they do business with the organization where a strike is in process. By refusing to buy from these other firms, union members hope to get them to stop purchasing from the company against which they are on strike. Boycotts of this type are illegal under the Taft-Hartley Act.

Political Action

While both the AFL and CIO concentrated on collective bargaining during their early years, they soon saw the need for political action. Over the years, this action has taken many forms. Lobbying is used to gain support for certain legislation that might affect the union. Although contributions in connection with national political campaigns are prohibited by law, political candidates or parties are endorsed by the unions when they appear to be friends of labor.

The Committee on Political Education (COPE) of the AFL-CIO is active in getting members out to vote and in getting them to become active in various political activities. In short, unions recognize the value of political influence and are quite active in the area at the present time.

Research and Public Relations

Unions must conduct research in various areas. For example, their leaders and representatives need information concerning wage rates, fringe benefits, employment levels, economic trends, legislative changes, productivity, labor costs, and a host of other items. Only by having such information can unions be fair and realistic in setting their goals and speak with authority at the bargaining table.

Most unions also believe in the importance of good public relations. Special staff groups at the local, state, and national levels are maintained to carry out this function. Books, pamphlets, newsletters, newspapers, movies, and other forms of materials are used to get the union story before the public.

Democratic Control and Leadership

While some unions have gained national attention because of bad practices, they represent only a very small part of the total union movement. Most unions have always followed a policy of democratic control and leadership. Both the AFL and CIO built their original organizations with the idea of granting member unions great degrees of freedom in handling their own affairs. This belief in democratic control is typical of the whole structure from the national to the local level.

Unions encourage the election of rank-and-file members to positions of leadership. Educational programs are available to help the union member prepare himself for advancement into offices of the union. Other educational programs are also made available by many national and local unions.

Special Codes of Ethical Practices have also been adopted by the AFL-CIO. These codes represent the Federation's thinking on democratic processes in the member unions. They include such categories as the proper handling of health and welfare funds, guidelines to prevent the improper use of other union funds, and procedures for the proper conduct of elections. These and other guides are designed to protect the member's rights as an individual in the organization.

UNDERSTANDING WHY WORKERS JOIN UNIONS

Workers may join or maintain their membership in a union for several different reasons. In some cases, the labor-management contract requires them to do so. In most cases, however, they join because they feel the union will try to see that more of their needs are met. In order to understand these needs, let us consider some of the common drives responsible for a person's willingness to work.

People are motivated by a desire to satisfy a number of needs which we may classify roughly as physiological, psychological, or sociological. Of these, the physiological or physical needs are the most obvious. In general, these needs are for food, clothing, and shelter. Psychological needs are shown by a drive for achievement, status, self-respect, and self-expression. Needs in this group are influenced by a person's relationship with other people, his philosophy of life, his social motivations, and his attitudes. A final classification is that of sociological or social needs. This group includes motives such as the need to belong (to be part of a group with similar interests), the need for love and affection (which is a secondary reward for working), the need for acceptance (in a society where being employed in some useful pursuit represents the respectable way of life), and the need for security (which goes further than the satisfaction of day-to-day requirements for food and shelter). Social needs stem primarily from our relationships with other people. They exist in us from very early in life. For example, when we think of our school days as carefree and enjoyable, we are not immediately aware of the fact that we were concerned with social needs. Yet a close examination of our behavior would show the presence of such needs. For example, why was it so important to be active in sports, to make good grades, to dress like other people, to learn the latest dances, or to have other people like us? The answer is simply that our behavior was directed toward satisfying certain social needs which continue throughout our lives.

From this brief discussion of human needs, supervisors should realize that workers join unions not because they are troublemakers or because they are not loyal to the company. They offer their services to the company in exchange for rewards that will help them satisfy certain physiological, psychological, and sociological needs. If employees feel that the company is not doing enough for them, they may ask for more money, shorter hours, or better working conditions. When they do, they believe that a united front is the *best* means of making their wishes known and getting some action. Workers often join a union in order to bargain collectively for those gains which will help them satisfy various needs. The following reasons for joining a union will serve to demonstrate this point.

To Gain Money and Security

Workers often join unions in order to seek, through collective bargaining, higher wages, shorter hours, better working conditions, fringe benefits, and job security.

To Keep a Job

Union shop agreements are a part of the union-management contract in a large number of cases, so that the worker is obliged to join the union after a specified number of days. He becomes a union member in order to keep his job.

To Have a Voice

Many workers want to speak out against management practices that appear to be unfair. They want a voice in determining wages, hours, working conditions, and so forth. If management does not give the worker an opportunity to express himself without danger of retribution, he may seek to gain such freedom of expression by joining the union.

To Be with the Group

Unions have a social attraction for some workers. Some employees join in order to be in a group with fellow workers and friends, to get together to enjoy picnics, dances, and other social events. The need to be part of the group and the desire to avoid pressures of disapproval often leads a member to join or to maintain membership even though he dislikes the union and what it stands for.

To Make a Contribution

Some workers are frustrated by the routine nature of their jobs, and may see little chance of advancement in the job itself. They may find, however, that they can become agents of the union and discover new ways of expressing themselves.

SUMMARY

The desire to obtain continued economic gains and a higher standard of living for members is the major objective of unions. They work for higher wage levels, payment for overtime, shorter hours, insurance coverage, pension plans, and other advantages affecting both pay and working conditions. In addition, unions seek work rules, legislation, and ways of providing more job security for their members.

Since unions seek maximum strength in their dealings with management, recognition and security are important to them. A union seeks to be recognized as the sole representative for a particular bargaining unit. In addition, unions seek various forms of security for themselves, such as the union shop, agency shop, maintenance of membership, and the dues checkoff.

To obtain their goals, unions employ a variety of practices. Collective bargaining is used to gain demands from management. If bargaining fails, tactics such as strikes, picketing, or boycotts may be used. On a long-term basis, unions work in the areas of political action and public relations.

Finally, we see that workers join unions for various reasons. Basically, they do so because the union offers to fill needs that have not been met by management. They may join to obtain more money and security, to keep a job, to have a voice in working conditions, to be with the group, or to make some contributions to the group's welfare.

QUESTIONS FOR DISCUSSION

1. Why is it important to understand union goals and practices?
2. How do union goals differ from those of management? In what areas are they the same? Discuss.
3. It appears that more and more unions are combining business and welfare activities. Is this true of the unions that you know? Why, or why not?
4. Can you think of any new or different goals that unions might pursue in the future?
5. Why do unions have economic gain and employee security as two of their major goals?
6. In what way does the dues checkoff provide a type of union security?
7. Why do unions sometimes use strikes, picketing, or boycotts in their dealings with management? Does management have any similar tactics to use in dealing with unions?
8. Unions have taken a more active role in political affairs since the 1930's. Is this also true of management?

9. Why do unions engage in public relations activities? Could management do more in this area? Why?

10. Why do workers join unions? Can you think of other reasons not discussed in this chapter?

(Note: See the Yaney and Rummler text, Chapter 2, Part 5, for exercises dealing with the topic of strikes. Also, see Chapter 4 of that text for an additional explanation of agency shop, boycotts, checkoffs, picketing, and union shop.)

SUGGESTED BIBLIOGRAPHY

Beach, Dale S. *Personnel: The Management of People at Work.* New York: The Macmillan Company, 1965, pp. 69-98.

Chruden, Herbert J., and Arthur W. Sherman. *Personnel Management.* Chicago: South-Western Publishing Company., 1963, pp. 485-503.

Dubin, Robert. *Working Union-Management Relations.* Englewood Cliffs, N.J.: Prentice-Hall, Inc., 1958, pp. 89-110.

Glos, Raymond E., and Harold A. Baker. *Introduction to Business.* Chicago: South-Western Publishing Company, 1967, pp. 363-379.

Yoder, Dale. *Personnel Management and Industrial Relations.* Englewood Cliffs, N.J.: Prentice-Hall, Inc., 1962, pp. 184-208.

3
Labor Legislation

Labor legislation provides guidelines for union and management groups to follow in their day-to-day relationships. While such legislation in the United States has developed primarily in the last thirty years, efforts to control unions and management can be traced through a longer period of time. We will examine these early efforts and the labor laws which now apply to union and management activities.

EARLY REGULATION OF UNIONS

The early regulation of unions in the United States was based upon English common law which had been adopted as the law of colonial America. Common law may be defined simply as the body of law which came about through court decisions made to settle certain disputes. These court decisions were recorded and served as guides for dealing with similar cases arising at later dates. Two doctrines from this body of law were often used to regulate union activities during the early 1800's. They were the Doctrine of Conspiracy and the Doctrine of Restraint of Trade.

Doctrine of Conspiracy

This doctrine was based on the idea that the organized efforts of a group might do more harm to society than the same actions carried out by individuals. In the United States, the doctrine was first applied in 1806 when a group of Philadelphia shoemakers was found guilty of organizing to raise wages. In similar cases a few years later certain New York and Pittsburgh shoemakers were found guilty of conspiracy for going on strike to obtain higher wages.

By the middle 1880's, American courts began to abandon the notion that workers were guilty of conspiracy solely because they organized in an attempt to obtain their demands. As a result, this doctrine was used less and less, and efforts were gradually directed toward developing different regulations.

Doctrine of Restraint of Trade

This doctrine is based on the idea that contracts or agreements are illegal if they tend to restrain trade or create a monopoly. In other words, the doctrine was directed toward preventing action that would hurt free competition. It was applied to unions when the courts believed that the actions of labor organizations would lead to a restraint of trade.

SHERMAN ANTITRUST ACT

The Sherman Antitrust Act was passed in 1890 to deal with contracts, agreements, or combinations that tended to restrain trade. The ideas included in the Act were certainly not new, based as they were on the earlier Doctrine of Restraint of Trade, but the Act did apply the doctrine to interstate commerce. As a result, the Federal Government became involved in administering the Act since it alone has control over interstate and foreign trade.

The Sherman Act did not mention labor organizations specifically, but was directed toward all combinations in restraint of trade. It was used against unions soon after it became law, however. The result was a series of court battles to determine whether unions actually were covered by the Act. Out of these court battles came one of the most important cases in American labor history. This was the famous Danbury Hatters case. In deciding this case, the U.S. Supreme Court held that certain actions of the Brotherhood of United Hatters of America were in restraint of interstate trade and commerce. As a result of this decision the union and its members were ordered to pay approximately $250,000 in damages.

Unions were unsure of their legal standing under the Act after the Supreme Court's ruling in the Danbury Hatters case. They saw the possibility of other damage suits which could cause serious financial problems for themselves and their members, and they set out on a campaign to obtain new legislation. These efforts played an important role in getting the Clayton Act passed in 1914.

CLAYTON ACT

This Act concerns the whole area of monopolies and combinations in restraint of trade. However, some sections of the Act apply specifically to labor. These sections resulted from the earlier efforts of unions to obtain more favorable labor legislation. Section 6 of the Act deserves special attention since it was designed to exclude labor organizations from coverage of the Sherman Act. Basically, this section states that nothing in the antitrust laws is to be interpreted as preventing the organization or operation of labor groups. In addition, it states that labor organizations shall not be held to be illegal combinations or conspiracies in restraint of trade.

Labor leaders were pleased with the passage of the Clayton Act since they felt that unions were no longer in danger of being placed under the coverage of antitrust laws. However, their satisfaction was soon replaced by new doubts and fears. Unions found themselves taken to court under various antitrust regulations, and several court decisions tended to weaken the language of the Clayton Act. Unions still had no clear definition of their legal status.

RAILWAY LABOR ACTS

During the late 1800's and early 1900's, several legislative acts were passed to deal with labor problems in the railroad industry. Of these, the Railway Labor Act of 1926 deserves special attention. This Act declares that employees shall have the right to bargain collectively through representatives of their own choice. The Act also prevents employers from interfering with either the formation of labor organizations or the choice of bargaining representatives. In addition, the yellow-dog contract was made illegal.

When all provisions of the Railway Labor Act are considered, a definite change in attitude toward labor unions can be seen. For the first time, there was a clear statement favoring collective bargaining. This new attitude which was to be reflected in later legislation, represented an important turning point in the history of American labor law.

NORRIS-LAGUARDIA ACT

One barrier that unions often faced during their early years was that of the injunction. Employers were able to obtain these court orders quite easily in most cases. As a result, injunctions were used to stop organizing efforts, strikes, picketing, boycotts, and other union activities. While the Clayton Act attempted to deal with the matter of injunctions, the effort had not been successful. Thus, it was not until the Norris-LaGuardia Act of 1932 that unions obtained relief from a widespread use of the court injunction.

Although the Norris-LaGuardia Act did not stop courts from issuing injunctions, it did spell out specific conditions under which they could be granted. In addition, by stating that yellow-dog contracts were illegal and not enforceable by law the Act removed another barrier to union growth. Employees could no longer be required to sign such contracts as a condition of employment.

Finally, the Norris-LaGuardia Act included a statement of policy which showed a continuing change in attitude toward organized labor. This statement made it clear that workers had the right to organize and to select their own bargaining representatives. This authorization marked the opening of a new era for unions in this country.

NATIONAL INDUSTRIAL RECOVERY ACT

This Act of 1933 grew out of efforts to pass legislation which would help our nation recover from the Great Depression. While the Act was not limited to labor-management relations, one of its sections was to play an important role in the development of later labor legislation. This was section 7 (a) which stated:

that employees shall have the right to organize and bargain collectively through representatives of their own choosing, and shall be free from the interference, restraint, or coercion of employers of labor, or their agents, in the designation of such representatives, or in self-organization or in other concerted activities for the purpose of collective bargaining . . . .

This statement was much stronger than those in either the Clayton Act or the Norris-La Guardia Act. The result was a clear indication of the federal government's decision to support collective bargaining activities.

The National Industrial Recovery Act also specified that workers could not be required to join a company union as a condition of employment and that employers would have to pay stated minimum wages while also meeting other conditions of employment as spelled out in the Act.

While the Act included some good points, there was a great deal of resistance to its provisions regulating production, wages, prices, hours, and labor-management relations. In an attempt to cure various business and economic ills, designers of the Act went too far. As a result, it was declared unconstitutional by the Supreme Court in 1935.

NATIONAL LABOR RELATIONS ACT

In 1935 shortly after the Supreme Court ruling which outlawed the National Industrial Recovery Act, the National Labor Relations Act, also known as the Wagner Act, was passed by Congress. Although it has been amended since that time, the Act remains as a cornerstone for the regulation of labor and management activities.

The Wagner Act continues the encouragement of collective bargaining as seen in the earlier Norris-La Guardia and National Industrial Recovery Acts. For example, it states that

> *employees shall have the right to self-organization, to form, join, or assist labor organizations, to bargain collectively through representatives of their own choosing, and to engage in concerted activities, for the purpose of collective bargaining or other mutual aid or protection.*

However, the Wagner Act continues by specifying a list of unfair labor practices for employers. This legislation makes it unlawful for an employer to do any of the following:

1. Interfere with employees in the exercise of their rights under the Act.
2. Dominate or interfere with the formation of any labor organization or contribute financial or other support to it.
3. Discriminate against union members in employment, or discharge workers because of union activity.
4. Discriminate against union members for filing charges under the Act.
5. Refuse to bargain collectively with the chosen representatives of employees.

The Act also established the National Labor Relations Board to administer the law. In carrying out its duties, the Board hears cases concerning unfair practices and takes action in defining bargaining units, certifying bargaining agents, and dealing with other matters covered by the Act.

From this brief discussion, we see that the Wagner Act was developed to protect labor and to encourage the growth of unions. Yet, the Act regulated the actions only of employers; union practices were not restricted in any way. As a result, some unions used their rights under the Act in an improper manner. For example, some unions refused to bargain with employers; others engaged in unlawful strikes or boycotts; in other cases, unions took advantage of their members by charging excessive dues and initiation fees. These and other abuses were largely responsible for the passage of the Taft-Hartley Act in 1947.

LABOR-MANAGEMENT RELATIONS ACT

This Act is also known as the Taft-Hartley Act. It resulted from several Congressional hearings where management witnesses indicated what they considered weaknesses of the Wagner Act. They pointed out that the Wagner Act restricted their behavior without placing a similar control on union activities. Union leaders, of course, felt that there was no need to change the Wagner Act. After the hearings Congress passed the Taft-Hartley bill. Although it was vetoed by President Truman, Congress overrode the veto. Thus the Taft-Hartley Act became a part of our present legislation in 1947.

The Taft-Hartley Act contains the same basic provisions as the Wagner Act concerning the right of workers to organize and bargain collectively. Only a few changes from those found in the Wagner Act were made in the sections about unfair labor practices for employers. The right of the National Labor Relations Board to administer the Act was also retained, but the number of board members was increased from three to five.

A major change provided by the Act involved the establishment of a list of unfair union practices. These include:

1. Coercing or restraining any employee exercising his rights under the Act.
2. Causing an employer to discriminate against an employee.
3. Refusing to bargain collectively with an employer.
4. Engaging in unlawful strikes or boycotts.
5. Requiring excessive initiation fees of members.
6. Requiring employers to pay for services which are not actually performed (known as feather-bedding).

One provision of the Act is of much current interest. This concerns the right of states to establish right-to-work laws. Under these laws, workers are not required to join a union as a condition of employment, but they may join if they choose to.

Emergency disputes are also covered by the Taft-Hartley Act. If a strike appears to be serious enough to endanger national health or safety, the Act provides for a number of steps which unions and employers must follow. In such cases, the President of the United States can appoint a board of inquiry to investigate the situation and file a report on the facts of the dispute. After studying the report, the President can ask the Attorney General to seek an injunction to prevent or halt the strike. If the court agrees that there is an emergency situation, the injunction is granted. A sixty-day waiting period then follows. Workers remain on their jobs during this time while attempts are made to settle the dispute. By providing for the cooling-off period, it is hoped that union and management groups will reconsider their actions and call off an actual or threatened strike. However, if they still fail to reach an agreement, a strike will result, since the Act provides only for the postponement of the strike. It does not grant any authority beyond that outlined above.

Additional provisions in the Taft-Hartley Act were directed toward removing Communists from union offices, requiring the filing of financial statements by the union, outlawing the closed shop, preventing strikes against the federal government, and limiting the political activities of unions. Through these and other changes, sponsors of the Taft-Hartley Act attempted to bring about a better balance of power in the field of labor-management relations.

LANDRUM-GRIFFIN ACT

Early in 1957, ten years after passage of the Taft-Hartley Act, a series of hearings on labor-management relations began. Conducted by a Select Committee appointed by the U.S. Senate, the hearings lasted for a year and a half. These events were televised and also received wide coverage on radio and in newspapers. The findings of the committee indicated that the officials of some labor unions were abusing their authority and failing to meet their responsibilities to union members. These and other practices led to the development of the Labor-Management Reporting and Disclosure Act of 1959, also known as the Landrum-Griffin Act.

Basically, the Landrum-Griffin Act deals with the internal affairs of unions. Provisions spell out the rights of union members among which we find:

1. Equal rights with all other members in nominations, voting, attending meetings, and participating in union activities.

2. Freedom to express their opinions and to meet with other union members for that purpose.
3. A voice in deciding on proposed increases in dues, initiation fees, or assessments.
4. Protection against being fined, suspended, or expelled from the union without first receiving a written list of charges, except in case of nonpayment of dues.
5. Freedom to *sue* the union or any of its officers, testify in any judicial, administrative, or legislative proceeding, or communicate with any legislator without interference from the union.

Rules and protective measures for conducting union elections are also included in the Act. The following specifications are made:

1. Elections must be by secret ballot,
2. Members have the right to nominate candidates,
3. Adequate notice of an election must be given,
4. Voting results for each candidate must be reported local by local, and
5. The union's constitution and bylaws will be used to govern the conduct of elections.

Unions are also required to file copies of their constitutions and bylaws with the Secretary of Labor and to file annual financial statements. These statements must report the salaries of all officers and employees of the union who receive more than $10,000 a year. Other sections of the law deal with the handling of union funds, the control of local unions by parent organizations, and a series of amendments to clarify and strengthen portions of the Taft-Hartley Act.

To summarize, the Landrum-Griffin Act serves to protect members from unfair and dishonest practices of union officers. In this respect, the Act represents an attempt to make unions more democratic by asserting that all members of a labor organization shall have equal rights and privileges to nominate, vote, attend meetings, and participate in union affairs. In addition, the Act can be viewed as another effort to provide a better balance of power between labor and management by restricting certain union activities while making others a matter of public record.

STATE LABOR LEGISLATION

While federal labor legislation is concerned with firms engaged in interstate commerce, state laws deal with companies operating within the various states. The authority to pass such laws comes from the police power vested in the states. This power gives a state the right to pass laws necessary to protect the health, safety, and well-being of people within the state. As a result, labor regulation in some states is more extensive than that provided by federal law. In general, state regulations center around legislation in one or more of the following areas:

1. Labor relations acts and anti-injunction laws,
2. Wage and hour regulations – including child-and female-labor laws,
3. Unemployment compensation,
4. Workmen's compensation,
5. Anti-discrimination laws,
6. Wage payments and working conditions.

Legislation in each of these areas has been developed to meet the needs of individual states. This has led to regulations which are usually different from state to state.

While state labor relations acts deal only with intrastate commerce, they are quite similar to the Wagner Act in many cases. For example, they set forth specific employee rights such as the right to organize and bargain collectively through representatives of their own choosing. In addition, the acts spell out certain unfair labor practices on the part of employers. Some states also identify unfair labor practices that apply to employees. Most states have labor relations boards to hear cases concerning unfair labor practices. The boards also define bargaining units, certify the bargaining representatives, and deal with other matters necessary in administering the laws. Other provisions of the various state laws are concerned with strikes, picketing, and boycotts. Right-to-work laws which give employees the right to decide whether or not they will join a union are found in several states. And, in some cases, annual reports must be filed by all unions in the state.

Many states also have anti-injunction laws similar to the Norris-LaGuardia Act. Kansas passed such a law in 1913; Utah and Minnesota did so in 1917. Other states soon followed with similar legislation. Thus, several states had regulations governing the granting of injunctions before the Norris-LaGuardia Act became law in 1932.

LABOR LEGISLATION AND THE SUPERVISOR

Each supervisor must acquire a knowledge of the legislation that regulates his day-to-day relationships with the union.

Although this takes time and effort, the benefits make it well worth while. For example, consider the following situations.

> Paul Black was a supervisor in a large midwestern manufacturing company. A fellow supervisor sat with Paul during lunch one day and began to talk about how much he disliked one of the employees in his section. During the conversation, the supervisor said he was going to transfer the employee to the night shift in order to get rid of him.
>
> Paul cautioned the other supervisor about transferring the worker. He knew the action would be regarded as discrimination against a union member. The result would be a charge of an unfair labor practice against the company.
>
> After some discussion, the supervisor saw that his action would be discriminatory, and that he could not offer definite facts to justify such a transfer. He decided that the best solution was for him to work toward eliminating the problem between himself and his subordinate.

In another situation, a general foreman prevented one of the supervisors in his section from committing an unfair labor practice. The company was just being organized and there was much discussion concerning the upcoming union election.

> The general foreman noticed that one of his supervisors was talking to the workers much more often than he had ever done in the past. After some investigation, he learned that the supervisor was telling the men to vote the union out or they would lose their jobs.
>
> The general foreman knew that the supervisor's actions would be interpreted as interference or coercion against the employees. He put a stop to the supervisor's interference and made it clear that the company would take

no action in such matters. His check on the supervisor prevented charges against the company of unfair labor practices.

The foregoing cases show why it is necessary that supervisors have a knowledge of labor legislation. You can check your own understanding of regulations governing industry and unions by taking Quiz 1 which you will find in the Appendix.

SUMMARY

In 1890, the Sherman Antitrust Act was passed to deal with contracts, agreements, or combinations that tended to restrain trade. While the Act included no specific mention of unions, court decisions soon applied its provisions to labor groups. As a result, unions were to remain uncertain of their legal status for almost 50 years.

The Clayton Act in 1914 represented the first attempt to exclude unions from antitrust laws. However, several court decisions which ruled that unions were covered by the Sherman Act tended to weaken the impact of this Act. Consequently, the legal standing of the unions was still not clearly defined.

A new attitude toward unions developed during the 1920's. This change was first seen in the Railway Labor Act of 1926 which included a clear statement favoring collective bargaining. Since that time an even more liberal attitude toward labor legislation has developed. Employees now have the right to organize and bargain collectively through their chosen representatives. However, certain obligations accompany this right, and the unions themselves must operate within the framework of guidelines established by legislation. Similarly, management is required to follow specified practices in their dealings with unions. Viewed in this manner, present labor laws attempt to provide for healthy relationships between labor and management.

QUESTIONS FOR DISCUSSION

1. Why were early unions often placed under the coverage of the Sherman Antitrust Act?
2. How did the Railway Labor Act influence later labor legislation?
3. In what way did the Norris-LaGuardia Act mark the beginning of a new era for unions in this country?
4. Was there any value from the National Industrial Recovery Act even though it was declared unconstitutional?
5. What might be considered as questionable about the way in which the Wagner Act sought to protect labor and to encourage the growth of unions?
6. How does the Taft-Hartley Act differ from the Wagner Act?
7. How does the Landrum-Griffin Act seek to provide more democracy for union members?
8. Why is it important for states to enact their own labor legislation?
9. Do you feel that our present labor legislation does a good job of regulating labor-management relations? Why?

10. What is meant by a "balance of power" between union and management groups?
11. What might the future bring in the way of federal labor legislation?
12. What would happen if all labor laws were wiped off the books?
13. How can you, as a supervisor, improve your knowledge and understanding of labor legislation?

SUGGESTED BIBLIOGRAPHY

Hastings, Paul G. *Fundamentals of Business Enterprise.* Princeton, N.J.: D. Van Nostrand Co., Inc., 1961, pp. 334-339.

Lester, Richard A. *Economics of Labor.* New York: The Macmillan Company, 1964, pp. 437-469.

Miernyk, William H. *The Economics of Labor and Collective Bargaining.* Boston: D.C. Heath and Company, 1965, pp. 113-138.

Pigors, Paul, and Charles A. Myers. *Personnel Administration.* New York: McGraw-Hill Book Co., Inc., 1965, pp. 200-206.

4
Understanding the Legislation

Labor legislation, as we have seen, provides guidelines for union and management groups to follow in their day-to-day relationships. The development of such guidelines resulted from efforts to produce a better balance of power between these two groups and thereby to insure healthy competition in union-management relations.

Unfortunately, the meaning of the legislation which governs union-management activities is not easy to grasp. The legislation is recorded in language that is difficult to read and understand. In addition, decisions by the National Labor Relations Board are continually introducing new interpretations of the legislation. Yet, each supervisor should have a general understanding of our present labor laws along with some idea of why certain legislation is necessary. And, of greater importance, the supervisor must have a good working knowledge of certain specific portions of the legislation. This is especially true of those clauses in the National Labor Relations Act (as amended) concerning unfair labor practices on the part of employers.

EMPLOYER UNFAIR LABOR PRACTICES

The National Labor Relations Act of 1935 spelled out five unfair labor practices on the part of employers. These were covered by amendments in the Taft-Hartley Act of 1947, and few changes were made. One point was made quite clear in the Taft-Hartley amendments. That is, employers are responsible for the actions of their supervisors in each of the areas concerned with unfair labor practices. Thus, the actions of a supervisor can lead to charges of unfair labor practices against his employer. Consequently, supervisors must know and understand their rights and limitations under each of the five clauses identifying unfair practices. Let us see what can and what cannot be done in these areas.

Interference, Restraint, and Coercion

In simple terms, the National Labor Relations Act (as amended) gives employees the right to form, join, or assist labor organizations, as well as the right to bargain collectively through their chosen representatives. The following section is designed to protect these rights by preventing interference, restraint, or coercion on the part of employers.

1. Employers cannot interfere with employees in the exercise of their rights to bargain collectively through their own representatives.

Since this section serves to protect employee rights granted by the Act, it is very broad in coverage. In fact, any unfair labor practice by an employer would be a violation of this section since he would be interfering with his employees as they exercised their rights. Keeping this point in mind, the following acts are cited as those that can or cannot be carried out under this section of the Act. The employer or you, as a supervisor,

CANNOT

a. Demote, transfer, or discharge employees because of their union activity.
b. Show preference to non-union employees in work assignments, etc.
c. Question employees about their union status.

d. Watch polls during an election in order to determine who is voting.

e. Attempt to influence union elections.

f. Favor one union over another.

g. Employ labor spies.

h. Attend union meetings for the purpose of spying on union members.

i. Spy on employees who are taking part in union activities.

j. Threaten employees with physical harm due to their union activities.

k. Do physical harm to employees engaged in union activities.

l. Make speeches or statements implying that any of the above will be done or that other actions leading to some loss of job security will be taken.

It is important to note that an unfair labor practice can be committed without direct action by either you or your employer. Any threats made through speeches or other statements can also lead to charges of unfair practice. For example, one company was found guilty of violating this section of the Act when a foreman asked an employee, "Wouldn't you rather have your job than be a union member without a job?" Thus, management personnel must not only be careful of what they do, but also mindful of what they say in their dealings with employees. The company or its management personnel

CAN

a. Urge employees not to unionize.

b. Express opinions of unions as long as no threats are involved and one union is not favored over others.

c. Pass out pamphlets criticizing unions.

d. Explain why employees are better off without unions.

e. Express opinions about union officers.

f. Let employees know they will not be discriminated against for union activities.

g. Offer counter arguments against union claims and charges.

As might be expected, extreme care must be exercised when any of the above acts is carried out. There is sometimes a very fine line between expressing an opinion and making threatening statements. If there is any doubt concerning matters in this area, the company's Industrial Relations Department should be consulted before action is taken.

Domination of Unions

This section of the Act is specifically directed toward preventing domination or control of company unions by management. This intent is clearly indicated in the section which follows:

2. Employers cannot dominate or interfere with the formation or administration of any labor organization, financially or in other ways.

Independent or company unions are not prevented, but the freedom of members to act without management pressure is carefully spelled out. The items below specify that the company or its management personnel

CANNOT

a. Oppose outside unions solely to gain a company union.

b. Offer or give financial support to a union or its representatives.

c. Request employees to sign cards or petitions where they indicate a preference for a company union.

d. Assist in organizing a company union, for example, by signing up members.

e. Threaten the job security of employees who do not show an interest in a company union.

f. Give to a company union privileges not shared by outside unions.

g. Interfere with, or hold, elections for purposes of choosing union officers.

Analyzing the items above, you can see that an unfair labor practice may result from either direct or indirect actions. If a supervisor makes direct statements favoring a company union, a clear case of influence can be seen. Moreover, even if a supervisor simply advises employees about their union membership when they ask him to, there is a possibility that this would constitute an unfair practice if the advice tended to favor a company union. In this respect, the National Labor Relations Board found one company in violation of this section when a foreman told an employee that a company union would be a "good deal" for the employees. Supervisors are wise to follow a "hands off" policy in this area. The company

CAN

a. Have a company union if it results from employee action and is not under the control or influence of management.

b. Treat all unions alike.

c. Tell employees they are free to join any organization without fear of discrimination on the company's part.

It is clear that the legislation does not prohibit company unions, but is designed to protect employees in exercising their right to form and join organizations of their own choosing.

Discrimination

In order to prevent discrimination against union members, the following clause is included in the Act:

3. Employers cannot discriminate against union members in hiring or other matters of employment, because of union activities.

When considering charges of an unfair practice under this section of the Act, the National Labor Relations Board is concerned with the motives behind certain actions. In other words, the Board tries to determine why certain actions were taken by the employer. For example, was the action taken against an employee because he was engaged in union activities? Or, was the action in line with established work rules or other procedures? To avoid being charged with an unfair labor practice, the company

CANNOT

a. Discharge an employee at the request of the union except for nonpayment of dues or initiation fees.

b. Threaten or discharge an employee for union activities.

c. Demote, transfer, or place an employee on less desirable jobs because he is a union member.

d. Refuse to hire a person, who meets the qualifications of a job, solely because he is a union member.

e. Refuse to hire an individual who is not a union member even though he is qualified for the job.

Discrimination would be clearly involved in the situations described above because the actions are based on whether or not an individual is or is not a union member rather than on established and well-defined business procedures. The company, on the other hand,

CAN

a. Have work rules, but they must be applied uniformly and without prejudice.

b. Discharge or discipline workers for reasons other than union activity.

c. Continue to assign preferred work, overtime, or shift preference to employees as long as there is no discrimination between union and non-union members.

d. Have a union-shop agreement where employees must join the union after a specified number of days.

To summarize, it should be made clear that the National Labor Relations Board does not attempt to remove a supervisor's freedom to enforce work rules and other regulations that are found in his section of the organization. However, these rules must be enforced without favoritism toward either union or non-union members. And, the supervisor should keep adequate records to show that his actions have been reasoned and impartial. Such records might indicate an employee's past violations of plant rules, past disciplinary actions taken for similar infractions, reasons for the actions that were taken, and the steps taken to follow up each case.

Discrimination for Filing Charges

This section of the Act gives employees the right to testify or file charges against an employer without fear of discharge or discrimination. In essence, the section states:

4. Employers cannot discriminate against union members for filing charges under the Act.

This section does not prevent employers from taking actions that are in line with normal operating policies and procedures. For example, employees can be discharged, disciplined, demoted, or transferred. However, such actions must not be taken for purposes of discriminating against the employee who has filed charges against an employer. If discrimination is threatened or actually takes place, it constitutes an unfair labor practice.

Refusal to Bargain

Under the Act, employees are free to bargain collectively through their chosen representatives. This right is protected by making it an unfair labor practice for an employer to refuse to bargain collectively with the representative of his employees. In simple terms, this section of the Act reads as follows:

5. Employers cannot refuse to bargain collectively with the chosen representatives of employees.

When considering charges of an unfair labor practice under this section of the Act, the National Labor Relations Board is primarily concerned with actions which fall into one of two areas: The company

CANNOT

a. Refuse to recognize representatives of the designated union for purposes of collective bargaining.
b. Fail or refuse to bargain in good faith.

Bargaining in good faith means basically that the employer is honestly attempting to reach an agreement with the union. In other words, his presence or the presence of company representatives at a series of meetings is not enough. So long as reasonable progress toward an agreement is being made, the company

CAN

a. Hear union proposals and make counter-offers.
b. Withhold negotiations with the union if there is genuine doubt as to whether the union is the chosen representative of the employees.
c. Tell the union why its offers are not acceptable to the company.

Employers can avoid charges of an unfair labor practice under this section by seeing that there is evidence of a desire to negotiate and reach an agreement.

ROLE OF THE NATIONAL LABOR RELATIONS BOARD (NLRB)

The National Labor Relations Act (as amended) is administered by the NLRB. This Board is composed of five members who are appointed by the President of the United States to serve for a period of five years. In addition, one person is appointed to serve as General Counsel for a period of four years. Usually the Board decides cases under the Act and the General Counsel deals with the prosecuting function. However, in either case, the role of the Board is to protect employees' rights as identified in the Act.

The Board determines bargaining units, conducts elections, certifies bargaining agents, establishes complaint procedures, conducts investigations, and issues cease and desist orders to stop unfair labor practices. In investigating and deciding cases, the Board helps to provide a better understanding of the legislation. This is especially true in those cases dealing with unfair labor practices. Through Board decisions, certain actions of unions and employers are judged to be either acceptable or unacceptable in various given areas. Although these cases arise from specific sets of circumstances, Board decisions tend to provide general guidelines when considered over a period of time. Union and management groups can then use this growing list of precedents in their attempts to understand the law and to avoid unfair labor practices.

ROLE OF THE U.S. DEPARTMENT OF LABOR

As previously discussed, labor legislation reflects the government's desire to protect certain rights of employees. However, before this attitude was widely expressed in the form of labor laws, the government was making efforts to protect employees. For example, a Bureau of Labor was created as early as 1884, and a Department of Commerce and Labor established in 1903. Such efforts resulted in an Act of Congress which created the U.S. Department of Labor in 1913. Since that time the Department of Labor has been working to improve the welfare of wage-earners: to improve working conditions, and to increase opportunities for profitable employment. In working toward these goals, the Department of Labor performs several functions under its various divisions.

Manpower Administration

This section of the Department of Labor is concerned with the training and development of human resources. Responsibilities for carrying out such actions may be assigned to Manpower Administration by legislative action or through directives from the Secretary of Labor. At the present time, this section includes the Bureau of Apprenticeship, Bureau of Employment Security, Neighborhood Youth Corps, and the Office of Manpower, Automation, and Training. Of these, the most important is the Bureau of Employment Security which carries out several important duties concerned with public employment offices and unemployment insurance programs.

Labor-Management Services Administration

Two offices in this section of the Department of Labor deserve special attention. The first is the Office of Labor-Management Welfare and Pension Reports. This office is responsible for administering those sections of the Landrum-Griffin Act and the Welfare and Pension Plans Disclosure Act which require unions and employers to file certain financial statements with the Department of Labor.

A second important office is that of Veterans' Re-employment Rights. This office handles the rights of veterans to the jobs that they held prior to entering military service.

Bureau of Labor Standards

A major purpose of this section is to coordinate federal and state agencies as they enforce various laws concerned with wages, hours, child labor, safety, and health. In this respect, the Bureau is active in developing standards related to child-labor regulations and other matters under the Fair Labor Standards Act. The Bureau also conducts research and provides information useful to various state groups dealing in the broad area of labor standards.

Bureau of Labor Statistics

The primary function of the Bureau of Labor Statistics is to gather information that is useful to government agencies, unions, employees, employers, and many other groups. This information is reported in various publications of the Bureau. Among these, the "Monthly Labor Review" is probably most widely known.

Information gathered by the Bureau includes data on the level of employment, employment trends, turnover of employees, size of the labor force, wages and hours, productivity, cost-of-living, labor-management relations, and industrial hazards. Such information is extremely valuable as an aid in determining wage rates, establishing recruitment-selection programs, collective bargaining, and in many other areas.

Wage-and-Hour and Public Contracts Divisions

These two divisions are responsible for administering the Fair Labor Standards Act and the Walsh-Healy Act which deals with wages and hours in work done under public contracts. The Divisions are concerned basically with matters such as the minimum wage, overtime pay, and child-labor regulations included in the Acts mentioned above.

In performing their functions, the Divisions investigate possible violations under the Acts and enforce the Acts where actual violations are identified. In addition, the Divisions are concerned with research and other matters related to wages and hours.

Women's Bureau

This Bureau exists to promote the status of women employed in the labor force. Working conditions, wages, employment trends, and other items are examined as they relate to wage-earning women. As a result of such studies, the Bureau is able to recommend standards of employment for women and can assist groups interested in working for the development of legislation affecting female workers.

ROLE OF AN INDUSTRIAL RELATIONS DEPARTMENT

The job of the Industrial Relations Department will vary from company to company. In some cases, it may be a fully staffed department involved with recruitment, selection, training, wage and salary administration, benefits and services, safety, recreation, labor relations, and other functions devoted to the management of personnel. In others, the department may be staffed by one person who can devote his time to only a few of these functions. However, in either case, the department most frequently serves in an advisory capacity to other portions of the organization.

The Industrial Relations Department can do much to assist supervisors in understanding pertinent legislation. For example, at least one person in the department should be thoroughly acquainted with all labor legislation and the NLRB decisions affecting the legislation. Such knowledge can be used to establish guidelines for supervisors to follow in order to prevent violations under current labor laws. In addition, the department can furnish information on other matters including: wage and hour legislation; civil rights legislation; procedures to follow in promotion, transfer, layoffs, and firing; provisions of the labor-management contract; and proper procedures to follow in handling grievances. In short, the Industrial Relations Department stands ready to offer advice and assistance in all areas of labor-management relations. For this reason, the wise supervisor consults the Industrial Relations Staff when he has any questions or doubts about his rights and responsibilities in this area.

SUMMARY

Each supervisor should have a general understanding of our present labor laws along with some idea of why certain legislation is necessary. Furthermore, the supervisor must have a good working knowledge of certain specific portions of the legislation. This is especially true of those clauses in the National Labor Relations Act (as amended) concerning unfair labor practices on the part of employees.

The Taft-Hartley Act made few changes in the five unfair labor practices of the Wagner Act. However, one point was made quite clear in the Taft-Hartley amendment: employers are responsible for the actions of their supervisors in each of the areas concerned with unfair labor practices. Thus, the actions of a supervisor can cause charges of unfair labor practice to be filed against his employer.

The National Labor Relations Act (as amended) gives employees the right to form, join, or assist labor organizations as well as the right to bargain collectively through their chosen representatives. The following sections of the Act are designed to protect these rights by preventing certain employer actions. In brief, employers cannot

1. Interfere with employees in the exercise of their rights to bargain collectively through their own representatives.
2. Dominate or interfere with the formation or administration of any labor organization, financially or in other ways.
3. Discriminate against union members in hiring or other matters of employment because of union activities.

4. Discriminate against union members for filing charges under the Act.
5. Refuse to bargain collectively with the chosen representatives of employees.

The National Labor Relations Board is responsible for administering the Act. In investigating and deciding cases, the Board helps to provide a better understanding of the legislation. This is especially true in those cases dealing with unfair labor practices. Although these cases arise from specific sets of circumstances, Board decisions handed down over a period of time tend to provide general guidelines. Union management groups can use them to prevent misunderstandings in the interpretation of law concerning unfair labor practices.

Acting in a staff capacity, the Industrial Relations Department of a company can do much to assist supervisors in understanding the legislation. Supervisors should take advantage of their special knowledge whenever they have questions or doubts concerning behavior which might come under provisions of union contracts or labor legislation.

Supervisors should also have some understanding of the role of the Department of Labor in various areas. Since its founding in 1913, the Department of Labor has worked for the welfare of wage earners, in particular to improve working conditions and to increase the opportunities for profitable employment.

QUESTIONS FOR DISCUSSION

1. Why are sections designed to prevent unfair labor practices included in the National Labor Relations Act?

2. Why should the supervisor be familiar with the sections of the National Labor Relations Act (as amended) which concern unfair labor practices on the part of both unions and employers?

3. Which of the following situations would be considered an unfair labor practice? Why? The situation where a supervisor

   a. Signs up members for a company union.

   b. Attends union meetings and writes down the names of all workers who are at the meeting.

   c. Stands at the polls during a union election and checks off the names of all workers who vote.

   d. Visits with each of his workers and asks them how they feel about the union.

   e. Passes out pamphlets which are critical of unions and union officers.

   f. Tells workers they will probably be replaced by machines if they join the union.

   g. Fires an employee who is a union member because he violated established work rules.

   h. Tells employees they should join a company union.

   i. Tells his subordinates to vote against the union if they want to keep their jobs.

   j. Gives all the good work assignments to non-union members.

   k. Tells his employees that he does not like unions.

   l. Asks his employees to sign a petition favoring a company union.

4. How can a supervisor's written records sometimes help to prevent charges of an unfair labor practice?
5. What is meant by bargaining in good faith?
6. What is the role of the National Labor Relations Board in administering the National Labor Relations Act (as amended)?
7. Of what value are decisions made by the National Labor Relations Board?
8. How can a company's Industrial Relations Department help supervisors gain a better understanding of labor legislation?
9. How can a company's Industrial Relations Department help supervisors prevent unfair labor practices?
10. What is the role of the U.S. Department of Labor?

(Note: For more practice in applying your knowledge of labor legislation, see the Yaney and Rummler text, Chapters 1 and 2.)

SUGGESTED BIBLIOGRAPHY

Cohen, Sanford. *Labor in the United States.* Columbus, Ohio: Charles E. Merrill Books, Inc., 1960, pp. 508-527.

Ecker, Paul, John MacRae, Vernon Ouellette, and Charles Telford. *Handbook for Supervisors.* Englewood Cliffs, N.J.: Prentice-Hall, Inc., 1959, pp. 26-32.

Jucius, Michael J. *Personnel Management.* Homewood, Illinois: Richard D. Irwin, Inc., 1967, pp. 457-461.

Keith, Lyman A., and Carlo E. Gubellini. *Introduction to Business Enterprise.* New York: McGraw-Hill Book Co., Inc., 1967, pp. 406-409.

Some Dos and Don'ts for Supervisors Under the Labor-Management Relations Act of 1947 and the Labor-Management Reporting and Disclosure Act of 1959. New York: National Association of Manufacturers, 1959.

5
Understanding the Contract

Working within the framework of labor legislation, union and management groups bargain over the terms, rules, and procedures which will guide them in their day-to-day relationships. The points finally agreed upon by both sides provide the content of the labor-management contract. At the present time, there are approximately 140,000 of these contracts operative in the United States.

To assist the supervisor in understanding labor-management agreements, we will begin by concentrating on the collective bargaining process, then discuss usual contract clauses, and finally, the supervisor's role in administering the contract.

THE COLLECTIVE BARGAINING PROCESS

Under the National Labor Relations Act (as amended), employees are granted the right to bargain collectively through their chosen representatives. Thus, after a union is named as the certified bargaining agent for a group of employees, both union and management must bargain on a continuous basis. In addition, current legislation requires that bargaining take place in the areas of wages, hours, and working conditions. Other issues that may be introduced at the bargaining table are determined by the parties involved.

Preparing to Bargain

The results of collective bargaining depend, to a great degree, upon the amount of time spent in preparing for the sessions. For instance, the representatives of both sides need detailed and factual information concerning wages, hours, working conditions, and a host of other items. Careful plans and proposals cannot be prepared without such information. And, in the absence of good plans, negotiations are often doomed to failure before they start.

Good planning begins with an analysis of facts related to the past and present and a forecast of future conditions. Information on grievances, disputes, past bargaining sessions, economic trends, political activity, and projected changes in the company and in the industry are especially important. Issues introduced by the union or by other unions in bargaining with other companies should also be considered since they point to topics that might be proposed.

Supervisors can play an important role in gathering information to be used in collective bargaining. For example, they should know how well the current contract is operating. They are aware of clauses in the contract which are difficult to administer. Their records on production, attendance, promotions, transfers, grievances, disciplinary action, and other matters provide valuable facts to be used in planning and conducting negotiations. It is essential that supervisors keep careful and accurate records in all these areas.

Bargaining

Since the formation of the American Federation of Labor, collective bargaining has been favored by unions as the best method for improving wages, hours, and other conditions of employment. However, this history has not produced a list of standard guidelines to be followed in the bargaining process. One bargaining situation differs from another. Management and union groups have their own individual goals, practices, and problems. So too do different companies and different industries have problems which vary from one to another. And all these things change with the times. Therefore the tactics of bargaining must also change as new situations arise.

Bargaining takes place between representatives of management on one side and the representatives of employees on the other. Management is frequently, but not necessarily, represented by the company's Director of Labor Relations. Other individuals may be chosen to represent management; the final decision depends on the size of the industrial relations staff and the qualifications of its members. The union is usually represented by its business agent or by a committee of union members and officers. In addition, both sides may be assisted by attorneys.

Although bargaining situations differ, the process is essentially the same. Proposals are introduced, discussed, and accepted or rejected. Counterproposals may be offered by either side as they seek to resolve their differences. The public hears about the bargaining sessions which result in deadlocks, but these are not typical. Most negotiations take only a short time and involve no work stoppages. In either case, however, the attitudes of the participants usually determine how difficult the bargaining process will be.

THE CONTRACT

Once union and management representatives have agreed on a contract, it is presented to the union members and to top management for final acceptance. If either side fails to approve the contract, their representatives are sent back to continue the negotiations. The contract which is finally accepted by both union and management is usually a complex legal agreement. While the form of the agreement varies from company to company and from industry to industry, there are some common features of most contracts. These are discussed below.

Recognition of the Union

The purpose of this clause is to indicate that management recognizes a given union as the sole bargaining agent for an identified unit of employees. In addition, the general items to be included in collective bargaining are usually noted. These points are indicated in the following example.

> The [Company] recognizes the [Union] as the exclusive bargaining representative of all employees in the defined bargaining unit for the purpose of collective bargaining in respect to rates of pay, wages, hours, and other conditions of employment, in accordance with the terms of this Agreement and within the provisions of the National Labor Relations Act, as amended.

Management's Rights

Management groups have often felt that unions were taking away some of their authority in operating the business. As the scope of collective bargaining has increased, this concern has become even more widespread. Thus, management frequently bargains for a clause in the contract which identifies the areas where it is free to act without joint action on the part of the union. In some cases, this clause specifies that management has the exclusive right to act in areas not covered by the contract. In others, management's rights might be identified as follows:

> The management of the plant and the direction of the working force: the right to hire, suspend, or discharge for just cause, to assign to jobs, to transfer employees in accordance with the Agreement, to increase and decrease the working force, to determine products to be handled, produced or manufactured, to schedule production, and to determine the methods, processes, means of production and handling are vested exclusively in the Company provided such exercise of authority will not be used for the purpose of discrimination against any employee covered by this Agreement.

Wages and Salaries

The clauses pertaining to wages and salaries are quite detailed and differ greatly from company to company. In general, however, they describe wage rates, salaries, methods of payment, bonuses, incentives, and so forth. If wage increases are determined by seniority, this information will also be included along with wage schedules and the methods of progression from one wage rate to another.

Hours of Work

This section of a contract usually specifies the regular working hours, rates for overtime pay, and shift schedules. In addition, holidays are identified, Sunday premium payments may be discussed, vacation provisions are outlined, and procedures concerning leaves of absence are often explained.

Fringe Benefits

Since World War II, fringe benefits have been included as a topic in most bargaining sessions. Common items under this category are hospital, surgical, and medical plans, sickness and accident insurance, life insurance, and pension programs. Sections of the contract dealing with fringe benefits are usually very detailed, since they deal with the specifics of each particular plan. For example, eligibility for certain programs, costs to the employee, extent of coverage, and other similar items are included in these sections of the agreement.

Grievance Procedure

This portion of the contract usually includes the definition of a grievance as agreed upon by labor and management. The following clause indicates such a definition.

> A grievance as mentioned herein shall be defined as any dispute or controversy arising out of the interpretation of, the application of, or compliance with the terms of this agreement.

Other clauses in this section usually refer to the prescribed method for handling grievances. Among other things, procedures for handling grievances are outlined.

Job Security

The basic clauses in this section are concerned with the areas of promotion, transfer, layoff, and recall. A seniority system may be set forth in this section. If so, seniority is discussed as related to such items as work assignments, choice of vacation times, and preferred shifts. In some cases, procedures for bidding and bumping* are often found in this portion of the contract.

No-Strike Clause

This clause is sometimes quite direct in stating that there will be no strikes or work stoppages during the term of the agreement. At other times, however, the statement is qualified to some extent. For example, consider the following:

> During the life of this Agreement, there shall be no strikes, work stoppages, slowdowns, or interruptions of production schedules caused by or sanctioned by the Union, and there shall be no lockouts by the Company until every peaceable means of settlement has been tried and exhausted.

Term of the Contract

As with other contracts, labor-management agreements specify the length of time during which the provisions of the contract will be in force. While many labor contracts are for one year, it is becoming more common for agreements to extend over a longer period of time. For example, the following clause indicates a three-year term.

> This Agreement dated September 15, 1966, shall remain in force and effect without change until 12:01 a.m., September 16, 1969. This Agreement shall automatically renew itself from year to year thereafter, unless at least

---

*Bidding occurs when job openings are posted so that employees within the company may apply for these positions before outside candidates are considered. Bumping takes place when a person of higher seniority requests the job, benefits, or accommodations of a person of lower seniority. Such a request may be made, for example, during periods of declining business when a man will prefer demotion to being laid off.

> sixty (60) calendar days and not more than ninety (90) days prior to September 15, 1969, or any September 15th thereafter, either party gives written notice to the other of its desire to amend, change, or terminate this Agreement. In the event of such notice, the Agreement will terminate on the next succeeding September 15th. The Agreement may be extended after such date by written agreement of the parties.

This section of the contract may also include provisions for a wage reopener. Under a reopener clause, either party may reopen negotiations on wages after a written notice has been filed with the other party. The following example illustrates the basic content of such a provision.

> During the term of this Agreement, either party shall have the right to reopen on the subject of wages by giving a sixty-(60)-day written notice of such intention to the other party.

ADMINISTERING THE CONTRACT

Once an agreement is reached, it must be administered on a day-to-day basis. Supervisors can play an important part in making this an easier task for all concerned. Their position in the organization puts them in close contact with employees and places on them a great responsibility in carrying out the provisions of the labor contract. They can get the company into trouble more quickly than any other group if they fail to meet this responsibility. Obviously, supervisors should study this area carefully.

Supervisors and the Contract

In order to administer the labor contract, supervisors must know precisely what it contains. No two agreements are exactly alike, but some clauses are rather common from one contract to another. If supervisors cannot understand certain portions of the contract, they should discuss them with other supervisors, with superiors, or with someone in the Industrial Relations Department. A supervisor should never feel that it is unimportant to understand every section of the contract. Such an attitude can lead to many problems which could have been prevented.

Supervisors and Management

Management can do much to help the supervisors to administer the labor contract properly. For example, they can call meetings in which the supervisors can be briefed on sections of the agreement. They can see that copies of the contract are distributed and arrangements made to handle questions that may arise. Such support is especially valuable when there are major changes from one contract to the next. In many instances a series of meetings are necessary if the supervisors are to realize maximum benefit. Meetings spread over a period of time provide more opportunity for a careful study, analysis, and discussion of specific items in the contract.

While management can help supervisors meet their responsibilities in administering the contract, supervisors can in turn help management in various ways. If clauses in the contract are not clear, they should communicate this fact to management. Likewise, when several grievances result from misinterpreting contract clauses, management should be informed. Only through such feedback can material be gathered for use in future bargaining sessions.

Supervisors and the Union

Since a labor agreement results from negotiations between union and management, it is reasonable to expect that the administration of the contract will also involve both parties. At this point, it is well to give some attention to the relationship between a supervisor and a shop steward. Both must attempt to satisfy many different people. Pressure is present in both jobs, and conflicts often arise between the two representatives. Yet both have somewhat similar goals even though they appear to be on different sides of the fence. Unfortunately, this point is often overlooked. The supervisor sometimes considers the shop steward a troublemaker who causes his job to be more difficult. For this reason, a supervisor may try to make the steward look bad whenever possible. The result is usually a relationship based on doubt, fear, anger, and emotion. Certainly, a minimum of benefit can come from such a relationship.

A good relationship between a supervisor and a steward must begin with an examination of their own attitudes. Attitudes are important because they affect the way we think, feel, or act toward a particular person or situation. For example, we hear what we want to hear. We shrug off new ideas that do not agree with our beliefs. We may remark that it won't work, or it has been tried before, or it is ok for others, but not for us.

In the area of labor-management relations, one supervisor may feel that work rules, grievance procedures, or other systems place too many limits on management. However, another supervisor may see such practices as important in developing better relationships. In other words, the first supervisor holds positive attitudes toward the same conditions that bother the second one so much. Efforts to establish a good relationship with local union representatives must begin with an analysis of ourselves. What are our attitudes in this area? Are we biased? To find out, complete the checklist on attitudes which you will find in Quiz 2 of the Appendix.

Many grievances can be prevented if the supervisor and shop steward will put forth a little extra effort to meet each other halfway. For example, consider the following case where such effort paid off for all parties concerned.

> Jack Poole was a machine maintenance man. He had been with the company for twelve years and was regarded as an excellent worker. His major responsibilities were the adjustment and repair of machinery in his department. He was also required to make daily inspections of the equipment.
>
> Several times each week, Jack had some time to kill after completing his inspections and making any repairs that were necessary. During such periods, Jack would usually spend his time reading hunting and fishing magazines. His supervisor had seen Jack reading on several occasions and had said nothing. Thus, Jack got in the habit of pulling out a magazine when things were going slow.
>
> Recently, however, Jack was reading when a machine went out of adjustment. Upon seeing the problem, Jack's supervisor chewed him out for neglecting his duties and told him he was suspended for a week without pay.
>
> Jack talked with his steward about the suspension and the two men then went to see Jack's supervisor. The steward argued that Jack was not neglecting his duties since his reading had nothing to do with the machine's going out of adjustment. In addition, management had said nothing about his reading in the past.
>
> Jack's supervisor stated that he was not getting paid for reading on the job. Furthermore, the other employees might try the same thing if Jack got by with it.
>
> After much discussion, the steward convinced the supervisor that the suspension was too strict since Jack had not been warned about his reading. He suggested

> that a warning notice in Jack's file would be an adequate remedy and that in the future Jack was to spend any extra time on additional inspection tours. The supervisor agreed to this proposal.

In summary, we see that all parties gained something when the supervisor and the steward were willing to meet each other halfway. Jack had a clearer definition of his job responsibilities. The company had prevented a competent employee from being penalized and unhappy, and management had learned of some areas where the plant rules were not clear. Finally, the union was able to demonstrate a continued willingness to help workers obtain a hearing through the grievance process. Consequently, the overall gain was the development of better labor-management relationships in this section of the company.

To work toward better relationships with the union, the supervisor should also recognize that the shop steward is both an employee and a union official. In other words, he wears two hats. While he is expected to meet the requirements of his job, he also has responsibilities to the union. The supervisor should recognize the fact that shop stewards are usually well prepared for their jobs. They are familiar with the operations and the people in the particular unit where they are assigned. They also have a thorough knowledge of the contract gained from union training programs and usually take their jobs very seriously. They are willing to do the extra work that will help them improve their performance as stewards. When supervisors are willing to show the same enthusiasm for their responsibilities in the labor-management area, they in turn make an important contribution to the development of better relationships with the union.

Supervisors and Themselves

A supervisor in any organization serves both management and employees. First, he must assist and gain the cooperation of subordinates and represent the workers in dealing with management. Second, his job is to see that his section produces efficiently and meets the schedules set by management. Needless to say, his task is a difficult one. Yet, the supervisor cannot escape his responsibility to protect the interests of both management and workers.

To carry out his job well, the supervisor must possess various types of knowledge. First, he needs a technical knowledge of the operations in his unit of the organization and a knowledge of labor relations. Second, he requires managerial knowledge in order to plan, organize, direct, coordinate, and control the activities over which he exercises authority. Finally, he must understand people. And, since people are the most important asset of an organization, this knowledge is extremely important.

Knowledge, of course, is not the only requirement a good supervisor must have. Experience is also necessary so that the supervisor develops techniques for applying his knowledge. Even knowledge and experience, however, are not all that is important. Their proper application depends on the attitudes held by the supervisor. Take, for example, his function in administering the labor-management contract. The time and money spent on training in this area is wasted unless the supervisor has healthy attitudes toward his responsibilities. The supervisor must consciously think about whether negative attitudes are influencing his performance. An understanding of himself and a willingness to change can improve relationships and result in both a happier atmosphere and improved production.

What about it? Do *you* need to do any work in this area? To find out, complete the checklist you will find in Quiz 3 of the Appendix.

SUMMARY

To understand the labor-management agreement, supervisors should have some understanding of the collective bargaining process, the various contract clauses, and the process of contract administration.

While collective bargaining has a long history in the United States, there are no standard guidelines to follow in the bargaining process. One bargaining situation differs from another. Management and union groups have their own individual goals, practices, and problems, all of which change with the times. As a result, the tactics of bargaining vary.

The contract which is finally accepted by both union and management is usually a complex legal agreement. While the form of the agreement varies from company to company, there are some common features of most contracts, clauses concerned with: (1) recognition of the union, (2) management's rights, (3) wages and salaries, (4) hours of work, (5) fringe benefits, (6) grievances, (7) job security, and (8) term of the contract.

Once an agreement is reached, it must be administered on a day-to-day basis. The supervisor plays an important part in carrying out this task. First, he must acquire a thorough knowledge of the contract as it affects the company and those under his supervision. Second, he must help management gather information for future bargaining sessions. Third, he must work to develop good relationships with union officers, especially the shop steward. Finally, the supervisor must seek to develop constructive attitudes toward his responsibilities in the labor-management area.

QUESTIONS FOR DISCUSSION

1. Why must the past, present, and future be considered when gathering information for use in collective bargaining?
2. How can you, as a supervisor, help management to gather information for use in bargaining sessions?
3. Discuss the records that you now keep. What ones could be used in collective bargaining? Are there others that might be of value if they were maintained?
4. Consider collective bargaining as it takes place in your organization. Do you feel that there are ways in which the process could be improved?
5. Refer to the union contract which affects you in your job. Consider each section of the contract. What clauses in it are similar to the ones discussed in this chapter? What ones are different?
6. Do you feel that management should bargain for a clause which identifies its rights? Why or why not?
7. Why should the grievance procedure be outlined in the contract?
8. Why should supervisors be familiar with the labor-management contract?

9. Why is contract administration an important responsibility of the supervisor?

10. As a supervisor, what can you do to become better prepared to administer the labor-management contract?

11. What can supervisors do to develop better relationships with shop stewards?

12. Why are a supervisor's attitudes important in contract administration?

(Note: For more information on the supervisor's role in the bargaining process, see the Yaney and Rummler text, *Labor Relations for the Supervisor,* Chapter 2, Section II, "Bargaining Questions for the Supervisor.")

SUGGESTED BIBLIOGRAPHY

Bittel, Lester R. *What Every Supervisor Should Know.* New York: McGraw-Hill Book Co., Inc., 1959, pp. 137-149.

Brown, Milon. *Effective Supervision.* New York: The Macmillan Company, 1956, pp. 193-207.

Famularo, J.J. *Supervisors in Action.* New York: McGraw-Hill Book Co., Inc., 1961, pp. 193-211.

Pfiffner, John M., and Fels, Marshall. *The Supervision of Personnel.* Englewood Cliffs, N.J.: Prentice-Hall, Inc., 1964, pp. 96-106.

Yoder, Dale. *Personnel Management and Industrial Relations.* Englewood Cliffs, N.J.: Prentice–Hall, Inc., 1962, pp. 252-267.

6
Handling Grievances

Dealing with grievances is one of the responsibilities of all supervisors. If this responsibility is fulfilled in a proper manner, companies benefit through savings in time and money. However, when handled unwisely, grievances lead to all sorts of trouble: wasted time, employee dissatisfaction, and a decrease in output, all of which add up to a loss of efficiency and money.

To provide supervisors with a better understanding of grievances, this chapter will touch on: (1) the general nature of grievances; (2) steps in a typical grievance process; (3) the role of arbitration; and (4) procedures for preventing or reducing grievances.

GENERAL NATURE OF GRIEVANCES

The term "grievance" means different things to different people. Some labor-management contracts refer to grievances as *controversies* or *disputes* arising from the application, interpretation, or violation of clauses in the agreement. At other times, the term is used in the same sense as a *gripe* or *complaint.* To understand these meanings, it is valuable to examine the various levels of worker dissatisfaction which lead to the ultimate filing of a grievance.

The primary level of employee dissatisfaction occurs when an individual is irritated or unhappy about something in the company, for example:

Perhaps he had to wait in line to get some tools he needed,

He could not get his vacation scheduled for the third week of June,

He was late to work because of a traffic jam in the parking lot,

The boss yelled at him yesterday, or

A night operator left his machine out of adjustment.

Of course, many other sources of irritation could be added to this list. The important thing, however, is that something in the work situation has upset the employee.

A secondary level of dissatisfaction is reached when the employee begins to complain about the irritation either to his boss or to fellow workers. At this stage, complaints are usually not put into writing. Instead, they represent attempts to "clear the air."

The final level of dissatisfaction occurs when the worker is so disturbed by a situation that he wants definite action. At this point, a written complaint is prepared for presentation to union and management representatives. The grievance becomes a formal, written complaint. Supervisors should not assume that all is well just because no written grievances are presented to them, however. Needless to say, workers can be quite irritated without putting their complaints in writing.

THE GRIEVANCE PROCESS

A basic purpose of the grievance process is to assure all parties that complaints will be handled in a fair and uniform manner. For example, if either party questions the contract, or the manner in which it is administered, the grievance process provides a method for settling the issue. In addition, the procedure serves as a valuable communication link between union officials, management, and employees.

The grievance process may be essentially an *open-door policy* in small organizations. Under this type of policy, employees are invited to discuss complaints with some members of management, frequently a member of the Personnel or Industrial Relations Department, in addition to their immediate supervisor.

The open-door policy is often favored by managers in smaller companies because they feel it provides a more informal method for dealing with matters which are disturbing employees. Managers in such companies feel that a more formal system would tend to destroy the friendly atmosphere which they try to maintain in their organizations.

Among larger firms, the open-door policy may also be used, but a more formal procedure is usually preferred. The structure of the organization is so large and complex that a more coordinated method for dealing with grievances becomes necessary. Moreover, in many larger organizations the labor-management contracts specify a formal grievance process. Typical steps in such a process are discussed in the following section.

Step One. The first step in a usual grievance process requires that employees present complaints to their immediate superior. In some cases, a union steward may represent an employee by introducing the complaint. While the complaint is often verbal at this stage, some contracts require that it be put into writing.

After a grievance has been presented, it is discussed between the supervisor and the employee. The employee is usually free to request that his shop steward be present at the meeting. After this preliminary discussion, the supervisor should attempt to do whatever is necessary to satisfy the complaint. However, if the supervisor cannot, or will not, take steps to eliminate the problem, the grievance can be taken to the next step in the process.

Step Two. At this point, the matter definitely becomes a formal grievance. It is in writing and is usually presented by either a union official or a grievance committee. In addition, a higher level of management is involved in hearing the grievance. The labor contract usually specifies who the management representative will be at this stage. He may be, for example, a general foreman or a section superintendent.

Step Three. If the employee is still dissatisfied with the action or lack of action at the second step, the matter is advanced to a third step. In many respects, taking a grievance to succeedingly higher levels of management is similar to taking a legal dispute through various courts until it finally reaches the U.S. Supreme Court.

When companies have an Industrial Relations Department, some member of that staff usually acts as management's representative at the third stage. However, other members of top management may sometimes act for the company. The union may be represented by a board of local union executives or by an officer from the national or international union.

Step Four. This final step in the grievance process usually calls for submission of the problem to an arbitrator. He hears the facts surrounding the grievance and issues a decision on the matter. The decision is binding on both parties, since union and management must have agreed, in advance, to accept and abide by the arbitrator's decision. Additional details of the arbitration process are included below.

ARBITRATION PROCESS

Issues taken to arbitration usually concern discipline, seniority in promotion or demotion, job classification, and work assignments. Other matters referred to arbitrators arise from disputes surrounding hours, pay, vacations, and management rights. Questions pertaining to both the process and the arbitrator's role are answered below.

Who Are the Arbitrators?

Arbitrators are usually college professors or lawyers. Most of them are listed with the American Arbitration Association and/or the Federal Mediation and Conciliation Service. To become a member of the American Arbitration Association, a prospective arbitrator must be asked to join; he cannot become a member at his own request.

While age, education, and experience vary among arbitrators, both union and management are in agreement about what they consider his most important qualification. Above everything, an arbitrator must have good judgment and be able to decide an issue on the basis of fact. The individual who becomes emotionally involved when issuing an award is not favored by either union or management.

Who Selects the Arbitrator?

Some contracts specify that union and management must agree on the choice of an arbitrator. Others call for a neutral party to make the choice. A third possibility combines the first two: union and management try to agree on the selection of an arbitrator, but ask a third party to make the choice if an agreement cannot be reached.

Either the American Arbitration Association or the Federal Mediation and Conciliation Service usually acts as the third party when union and management cannot agree on an arbitrator. Upon request, either agency will send a list of qualified individuals from which union and management can make their choice; either agency will select an arbitrator if asked to do so by the parties involved.

What Are the Arbitrator's Duties?

Basically, an arbitrator holds a hearing at which the facts surrounding a grievance are introduced. Both parties present their arguments along with supporting evidence. In addition, the parties usually have an opportunity to question each other as well as any witnesses who might have information bearing on the case.

The arbitrator listens to the arguments of both sides and may ask questions in order to obtain a better understanding of the evidence. He must then consider the facts of the case and prepare his decision. In doing so, the arbitrator cannot modify or change the labor-management contract. His decision must be made in accordance with the prevailing agreement. Thus, while a grievance may point out the need for some change in the contract, alterations can be made only during future negotiations between union and management. The arbitrator has no authority in this area.

How Much Are Arbitrators Paid?

While figures vary, the average fee for an arbitrator's services is between \$100 and \$150 a day for the time spent in hearing a case plus the time spent in preparing the decision. The fee may, or may not, include expenses.

Union and management usually agree to share the costs of arbitration, although some contracts may call for other arrangements.

What Happens to the Arbitrator's Decision?

Since both management and the union must agree, in advance, to accept the arbitrator's decision as final and binding, and since this agreement has been included as a clause in the contract, the arbitrator's judgment cannot be overruled. In fact, his decision can be enforced through court action since it results from a contractual agreement between the two parties.

Once a decision has been issued by an arbitrator, it is frequently included in various publications such as the *American Arbitration Reports.* These decisions are widely read and may be considered by other arbitrators as they deal with similar situations. Arbitration decisions do not become precedents, however, such as do rulings handed down in a court of law.

PREVENTING OR REDUCING GRIEVANCES

The establishment of a formal grievance process is necessary before employee complaints can be handled in a systematic, factual, and objective manner. However, the development of such a process is only the first step in building an effective program for dealing with grievances. In the final analysis, the prevention or reduction of grievances depends on how supervisors and other management personnel deal with them before, or after, they begin moving through the various steps of the grievance process.

To be most effective in meeting their responsibility in this area, supervisors should consider the following points.

Be a Problem Solver

When handling grievances, a supervisor can be either a problem or a problem solver. If he attempts to disregard his responsibility for dealing with grievances, he definitely becomes a problem. For example, he may pass the buck, argue with employees who have grievances, or look for some easy way out. On the other hand, he can accomplish a great deal by using proven guidelines and following the steps we'll now discuss.

Define the Problem. This step calls for the isolation of the *true* problem. Some grievances are never settled because the primary source of irritation is not uncovered. For example, a supervisor was frequently approached by a worker who complained that his wage rate was not in line with other jobs in the department. The complaints continued even after the supervisor had explained the wage structure, seniority provisions, and so forth. Finally, during a long discussion, the truth came out. The employee was not concerned about his wage rate. His anxiety stemmed from worry about keeping his job, since he had heard rumors about new equipment which was to be installed in his department. After being reassured about job security and his relationship with the supervisor, the employee's complaints stopped.

The example presented above is not an isolated case. Many stated grievances are cover-ups for other things which bother employees. In this respect, a grievance is like an iceberg. While an observer can see that part which is above the water, there is a larger part which cannot be seen below the surface. So too, with grievances, the wise supervisor must constantly look for causes which lie below the surface. Failure to do so can lead to continued or more serious grievances in the future.

Get the Facts. Sometimes facts must be gathered in order to clearly define the actual nature of a grievance. Accumulating facts must frequently be continued after the true grievance has been identified. Without reliable knowledge the supervisor cannot hope to settle the issue in a satisfactory manner.

The fact-gathering process usually begins when a grievance is discussed with the employee who has presented it. One precaution you, as the supervisor, must observe during such discussion can be expressed in two words—*don't argue.* Arguments do not lead to fruitful results. Instead, a situation develops where each party is trying to convince the other that he is wrong. Emotions run high and both sides start to put things on a personal basis. Any chance of their studying the problem objectively disappears, and the situation usually becomes worse rather than better.

To identify the facts related to a particular grievance, the supervisor must seek information which answers such questions as:

What is the problem?

Where did it occur?

Who was involved?

When did it start?

Why is it a problem?

In gathering such information, other questions must also be asked. For instance,

> Were there any observers?
>
> Has it happened before?
>
> Have other supervisors experienced similar situations?
>
> Are there any records which can shed light on the matter?

While many other questions can be raised, these examples show the need for information from various sources. As might be expected, this step in problem solving probably requires more time than any other. The time is well spent if it leads to a satisfactory solution and the prevention of similar problems in the future.

Select Possible Solutions. After all the facts related to the situation have been obtained and the true nature of a grievance has been determined, the supervisor can begin to select possible solutions. He may discuss the matter with his superior, other members of management, or other supervisors. Experience may show how similar cases were handled in the past.

Evaluate the Possible Solutions. The supervisor should consider all possible solutions which fit the facts of the situation at hand. Snap judgments should be avoided; they often create the impression that the supervisor has a careless and indifferent attitude toward grievances. The supervisor can avoid some trial and error by studying the situation and using his best judgment, but he cannot know whether he has selected an appropriate solution until it has been put into practice.

Choose the Solution and Put It into Action. Once the decision is made and the solution chosen, action must be taken. While this would seem to be only common sense, the benefits of good problem solving are sometimes destroyed by a lack of prompt action. Employees expect something to be done when they file a grievance. Why look for more data even though you know you have enough? Why try to pass the buck when an examination of the facts shows you are at fault? Why refuse to say "No," if the situation calls for such an answer? In other words, why postpone action when the facts show what needs to be done? If you were ill and visited a doctor for a thorough physical examination, would you expect to wait six weeks before he told you what to do? While this is a somewhat exaggerated example, it does show the need for prompt action in cases where an individual is personally and deeply concerned.

After the solution has been put into action, the supervisor should check to see whether the employee is satisfied. Is he still irritated? How is he taking the decision? These and other questions must be asked. Only through a follow-up can the supervisor see whether any additional action is required.

Other Guides

While problem solving is essential for the prevention or reduction of grievances, other guides are also useful. Some of these are considered in the following sections.

Don't Close the Door. All supervisors must indicate a willingness to hear employee complaints. In general, this means that each supervisor must maintain his own open-door policy. Words alone are not enough: the good supervisor also makes it known through his actions that employees are welcome to discuss their grievances with him. If he doesn't, employees often feel an implied lack of sympathy and are reluctant to speak freely with him. As a result, minor complaints sometimes grow out of proportion very rapidly.

Listen With Both Ears. Above everything, a supervisor must indicate a sincere desire to hear an employee's story. Your sincerity is best demonstrated through good listening. Let the employee tell the whole story. Be careful not to interrupt him unless it is absolutely necessary to clarify certain points. Don't try to finish off some paperwork while the employee talks. In short, make him the center of interest by giving him your full attention.

Use a Two-Way Mirror. Too frequently we see things from only our own point of view. Unfortunately, management is sometimes guilty of this in their handling of grievances. The result is that employees often feel that a supervisor is unfair and has a closed mind. To forestall such feelings, the supervisor should make an honest attempt to consider *all* points of view that are related to a particular grievance, and make it clear to the worker that he is doing so.

A Note Today Saves Time Tomorrow. Records are extremely valuable when dealing with grievances. Have there been similar complaints in the past? If so, what action was taken? How did it work out? Has a certain employee filed grievances in the past? Questions like these can often be answered if the supervisor has maintained careful records.

The time required to maintain records on grievances is well spent. A few minutes devoted to making notes about an employee's grievance may save many minutes or hours when dealing with other complaints in the future.

LEARNING FROM GRIEVANCES

Supervisors should view each grievance as an opportunity to learn. All grievances arise from some set of conditions which irritate a worker. Why not learn from each situation? Why be content with handling grievances? Why not try to prevent them? Make a search for those irritations on each worker's job which might lead to grievances and help remove them before they lead to trouble. In addition, once the cause of a particular grievance has been identified, remove that cause and do your best to keep it from returning at a later date. Of course, taking measures to prevent grievances requires continued efforts over a long period of time, but the results are well worth the effort.

To assist you in handling and preventing grievances, a check-list is included in Quiz 4 of the Appendix.

SUMMARY

A formal process for handling employee grievances is designed to assure both parties that complaints will be administered in a fair and uniform manner. In addition, the procedure serves as a valuable communication link between union officials, management, and employees.

The supervisor can use certain guidelines to become a good problem solver. These include:

1. Defining the problem,
2. Obtaining the facts,

3. Selecting possible solutions,
4. Evaluating the possible solutions, and
5. Choosing the best solution and putting it into action.

As another aspect of his role in dealing with personnel problems, the supervisor must make it known through his actions that employees are welcome to discuss their grievances with him. Good listening habits should be cultivated, since careful listening indicates a sincere desire to hear an employee's story. The wise supervisor not only tries to consider the employee's point of view, but he makes it clear to the worker that he is doing so. He must think about how he would act if he were in the employee's position.

The supervisor should appreciate the value of good records as an aid in solving grievances, and see that records are carefully maintained for the future. The supervisor should also view each grievance as an opportunity to learn. Grievances arise from some set of conditions which irritate a worker. The supervisor should search for other possible sources of irritation and remove them before they lead to trouble. While success requires awareness, time, and effort on the part of the supervisor, the results justify this, and in the long run benefit not only the worker, but the company and the supervisor himself.

QUESTIONS FOR DISCUSSION

1. What steps are included in your company's grievance process? If there is no formal process, how are grievances handled?

2. Do *you,* as a supervisor, use anything like an open-door policy?
   a. If so, what are the benefits of such a policy?
   b. Are there any disadvantages?
3. What can a company do to reduce the number of grievances which go to arbitration?
4. How do *you* attempt to determine the true nature of a grievance?
5. What practices do you follow in trying to prevent or reduce grievances?
   a. Which of these practices do you consider the most important?
   b. Could you do anything else?
6. Can a good relationship with shop steward help to prevent or reduce grievances? How?
7. A worker complains to you about gas fumes in his work area. You report the complaint to the maintenance department. Maintenance finds a faulty vent fan and corrects the situation. However, the worker keeps coming to you with the same complaint even though later inspections by maintenance show no fumes.

   What would you do if the worker continued to present this same complaint?
8. A supervisor has what he calls an open-door policy. Workers are invited to discuss their grievances with him at any time. However, there are frequent interruptions during such discussions. The phone rings, other workers come in to ask questions, or the supervisor has some

papers to sign while the plant messenger is waiting. In spite of these interruptions, this supervisor feels he is showing a definite interest in the problems of his employees.

a. Do you agree with the supervisor?

b. How could the situation be improved?

9. A worker is discussing a grievance with his supervisor. Before the worker finishes his side of the story, he is interrupted by the supervisor, who says, "Go see personnel. I can't do anything about it—it's out of my area."

a. Was there anything wrong with the supervisor's approach?

b. Why?

10. At the end of the shift, Tom complains to his supervisor that two fellow workers have been leaving their jobs early in order to beat the rush in the parking lot. Tom goes on to say that the two employees use the excuse that they have to return some tools before quitting time. "Well, I'll see about that," says the supervisor. The next morning, each of the two workers find the following note attached to his time card:

"Working hours are 7:30 to 4:00. Continued violation of the rules will lead to disciplinary action."

a. What do you think of the supervisor's action?

b. How would you have handled the case?

11. An employee has been late to work five times in the last two weeks. He keeps telling the boss that his wife is ill and that he has to make daily arrangements for

his mother-in-law to stay with her. This makes him late to work. When the supervisor checks into the matter, he finds that the employee's wife is in very good health, but that the couple are apparently having problems with their marriage. Nevertheless, the supervisor fires the employee on the spot.

What would you have done?

12. Joe is a practical joker who likes to tease his fellow workers. His supervisor has talked to him about the jokes, but has not taken any other action.

    Recently, Joe tossed a small firecracker under the feet of another employee. The noise was not loud, but it upset the other worker. He grabbed a bolt from his assembly table and threw it at Joe. The bolt missed Joe, but went crashing through a window.

    The supervisor fired both workers when he heard of the incident. The two workers filed grievances with their shop steward.

    a. Would you have handled the situation in the same manner?

    b. Why or why not?

(Note: For more practice in grievance handling, see the Yaney-Rummler text, Chapter 3.)

SUGGESTED BIBLIOGRAPHY

Gellerman, Saul W. *The Management of Human Relations.* New York: Holt, Rinehart and Winston, 1966, pp. 74-83.

Heckmann, I.L., and S.G. Huneryager. *Management of the Personnel Function.* Columbus, Ohio: Charles E. Merrill Books, Inc., 1962, pp. 429-447.

Johnson, Charles W. *The Supervisor – Key Management.* Englewood Cliffs, N.J.: Prentice-Hall, Inc., 1960, pp. 90-99.

Jucius, Michael J. *Personnel Management.* Homewood, Illinois: Richard D. Irwin, Inc., 1967, pp. 470-487.

Kalsem, Palmer J. *Practical Supervision.* New York: McGraw-Hill Book Co., Inc., 1945, pp. 42-53.

Appendix

QUIZ 1

LABOR LEGISLATION

(To be administered at the close of Chapter 3)

Circle T for true and F for false.

1. A supervisor can threaten to punch an employee in the nose for his union activities as long as he doesn't carry out his threat. T F
2. Since you are a member of management, you can ask employees to sign petitions to indicate a preference for a company union. T F
3. As a supervisor, you are free to watch the polls during a union election in order to determine who is voting. T F
4. You are free to assist employees in organizing a company union. T F
5. You can fire an employee for his union activities in order to keep the union out of your company. T F
6. In order to discourage unionization, a supervisor can transfer employees to less desirable jobs because of their union activities. T F
7. It doesn't hurt if you pressure employees into joining a company union. T F
8. You can ask employees if they are going to vote for the union in a future election. T F

9. It's o.k. for you to tell employees that the company will give financial support to a company union.
T F

10. In order to keep union members out of your company, you can always refuse to hire them.

SCORING

Give yourself five points for each time you circled "false." If your score is 40 or above, you are doing fine. However, this is only a short quiz, so don't feel too sure of yourself. Read Chapter 4 to provide an additional check on your knowledge of the legislation.

A score of less than 40 indicates that you need to work on improving your knowledge of the legislation. Study Chapter 4 carefully and then go through this quiz again before answering the questions at the end of that chapter.

QUIZ 2

ATTITUDES TOWARD SHOP STEWARDS

(To be administered at the close of Chapter 5)

1. Do you know the name of the shop steward in your area of operation? Yes___No___
2. Do you understand the shop steward's role in the union's organizational structure? Yes___No___
3. Do you have confidence in the ability of the steward in your area? Yes___No___
4. Do you try to understand the shop steward's problems? Yes___No___
5. Do you try to see things from the steward's point of view? Yes___No___
6. Do you try to avoid jumping to conclusions when talking with the shop steward? Yes___No___
7. Do you try to be fair in your dealings with the shop steward? Yes___No___
8. Do you welcome suggestions from the steward? Yes___No___
9. Do you take time to discuss the union contract with the shop steward? Yes___No___
10. Do you discuss methods for preventing grievances with the shop steward? Yes___No___

11. Do you listen interestedly and patiently when the steward talks with you? Yes___No___

12. Do you trust the shop steward with whom you must work? Yes___No___

13. Do you feel that the shop steward can help make your job easier? Yes___No___

14. Do you feel that the shop steward makes reasonable requests in his dealings with you? Yes___No___

15. Do you know the union-management contract as well as the shop steward in your area? Yes___No___

16. Do you have an open mind concerning unions and their actions? Yes___No___

17. Do you encourage a free and open discussion of opinion in your contacts with the steward? Yes___No___

18. Do you ever ask the shop steward for advice concerning problem employees? Yes___No___

19. Do you try to develop a good working relationship with the shop steward in your area? Yes___No___

20. Do you keep your emotions under control in your dealings with the shop steward? Yes___No___

SCORING

Give yourself five points for each "yes" answer.

90-100	Excellent! You have developed good attitudes toward the shop steward.
80- 89	Good, but work on some of the "no" answers to raise your score.
70- 79	Fair. You should plan a definite course of action to correct your weak points.
60- 69	Danger! Get to work on your weaknesses right now.
0- 59	Poor. Talk with your boss, other supervisors, or to someone in Industrial Relations. Unless you begin immediate action to improve your attitudes, anything can happen.

QUIZ 3

ATTITUDES TOWARD CONTRACT ADMINISTRATION

(To be administered at the close of Chapter 5)

Circle T for true and F for false.

1. Contract administration is a waste of time. In fact, employees should not be allowed to join a union. T F

2. Most union members are never happy, so I shouldn't have to worry about knowing their rights as spelled out in the contract. They will gripe in spite of anything I do. T F

3. It is not my job to know the labor-management contract which covers my subordinates. The Industrial Relations Department has that responsibility. T F

4. No one can understand a union contract unless he is a Philadelphia lawyer. T F

5. Shop stewards are always looking for ways of getting around clauses in the labor-management agreement. T F

6. Each employee complaint is actually an attempt to get something from management. T F

7. The Industrial Relations Department isn't interested in my problems. Why ask them anything about the contract? T F

8. If I don't understand some clauses in the contract, I shouldn't worry since they will probably be changed in the next contract anyway. T F

9. Contracts give shop stewards more excuses to file grievances. T F

10. If I get my section's work done, management shouldn't worry about how well I get along with the union. T F

11. All labor-management contracts favor the union. T F

12. Grievance procedures are a waste of time. If employees are unhappy about something, they should quit. T F

13. The labor-management contract is of no value to me as a supervisor. T F

14. The concept of job security is ridiculous. Employees work harder when they are afraid of losing their jobs. T F

15. Why should I furnish management with information to use in collective bargaining? The union always gets what it wants anyway, so my information is of no value to anyone. T F

SCORING

Give yourself five points for each time you circled "false."

65 - 75 Excellent! You have developed good attitudes toward contract administration.

55 - 64 Good, but work on some of the attitudes that led you to circle T.

45 - 54 Fair. Your answers indicate some negative attitudes. Reconsider those statements and analyze your reactions.

35 - 44 Danger! Take a long look at those T answers; your negative attitudes are showing. Do some serious thinking about yourself.

0 - 34 Poor. Your attitudes are very negative. Get to work on improving them right now. Devote a lot of time to thinking about those T answers. Compare your ideas with those of other supervisors.

QUIZ 4

HANDLING GRIEVANCES

(To be administered at the close of Chapter 6)

Checklist

1. I take time to look for the *true* problem behind all grievances that are filed. _____
2. I ask myself the following questions:
   a. Where did the problem occur? _____
   b. When did the problem occur? _____
   c. Who was involved in the problem? _____
   d. Why is it a problem? _____
3. In choosing possible solutions for dealing with a grievance, my procedure is to:
   a. Re-examine the nature of the grievance. _____
   b. Look at the grievance from the employee's point of view. _____
   c. Talk with other supervisors about the grievance when I feel they can offer some advice. _____
   d. Consider past cases of a similar nature. _____
4. In evaluating each possible solution, my procedure is to:
   a. Avoid spur-of-the-moment decisions. _____
   b. Weigh the possible results of each alternative. _____
   c. Consider how each solution might prevent similar grievances in the future. _____

Checklist

5. Once a solution has been selected, my procedure is to:
   a. Put it into action without delay. _____
   b. Avoid passing the buck. _____
   c. Make a note of the action that was taken. _____
   d. Make plans to follow up on the action to see how well it is working. _____

SCORING

No scoring is necessary. This checklist simply offers a convenient way for you to assess your own attitudes and procedures.